to Margaret
from John
with love

May 1986

Also available from Collins
as a Fount Paperback

WHY I AM STILL AN ANGLICAN

*Sister Anna, A. N. Wilson,
Roger Hooker, John Whale,
Tommy Dingsdale MBE,
Frank Field MP, John V. Taylor*

edited by Tobias Churton

COLLINS
8 Grafton Street, London W1
1986

William Collins Sons & Co. Ltd
London · Glasgow · Sydney · Auckland
Toronto · Johannesburg

BRITISH LIBRARY CATALOGUING IN PUBLICATION DATA

Why I am still an Anglican.
1. Christian life—Anglican authors
2. Faith
I. Churton, Toby   II. Anna, Sister
248.4'83   BV4501.2
ISBN 0 00 217502 9

Photoset in Linotron Bembo by
Rowland Phototypesetting Ltd
Bury St Edmunds, Suffolk
Made and printed in Great Britain by
William Collins Sons & Co. Ltd, Glasgow

Contents

INTRODUCTION

WE LIVE IN a strange world because there is a part of us which is a stranger to the world. Jesus came into the world as our friend and yet was treated as we treat strangers. When we expose our strangeness we form religions – an activity quite peculiar to mankind. Do dolphins worship? No, but they do sing and much of our worship is made in the songs we carry in our hearts. But the voice raised in song is rare today, and worship rarer still. Do we believe we have everything – or is it that we want everything? There is a school which teaches that religion is a matter of indifference, indeed, that we should be more *natural* without it – more like the dolphins to swim and dive in the wake of progress.

The contributors to this collection of essays do not share this view. What they do share is that they are ready to be called Anglican Christians. It has been argued that this nomenclature is in fact all that Anglicans do share – that the Anglican Church is a false enclave of individual seekers worshipping in the Church of England as an act of convenience. The argument continues to assert that those who become acutely sensitive to this must pack their spiritual bags and hot-foot-it to the Roman Catholic Church 'before it is too late'. In other words, Anglicans make a compromise of commitment, for the One True God can only lead to One True Church. Pluralism of any kind is judged in this view to be pernicious. Such a view can have little claim to be related to the reality of human life, for a cosmic pluralism is the way of creation. But can there be diversity without division? 'Reality leaves a lot to the Imagination' said an inspired man – so perhaps the question is impertinent.

However *this* question may have a solution. A parable from nature may give us a clue to it. The simplest form of reproduction is that of the asexual division of cells, the result of which is a mere repetition, indeed a *cloning*, of the preceding cell. In the human reproductive events, diversity or *new* life is achieved through the necessary sharing in mutual interaction of divided cells – just as the human Christ was made possible through a new reproductive diversity: born of the Holy Spirit and of flesh, according to the will of God and the prayer of humanity. There can *be* no diversity without a division – nor can there be new creation without diversity.

Here is a book containing the thoughts and experiences of seven Anglicans, and the reader must judge for himself or herself whether they share anything but the paper they are written on.

They write in answer to the question: 'Why are you *still* an Anglican?' Why have they not laid down the burden of faith in times when it is sung 'the more I see the less I believe'? Why not then call the book 'Why I am still a Christian'? It is not called so because this book is essentially a study of *character,* and 'Anglican' is, I think, better seen as a description of character than of belief though beliefs are bound to character, and when it is asked 'What do Anglicans actually believe?' we might reply 'as much depends on the character of the believer as on the belief of the character'! For that reason I asked the contributors to offer as *personal* an essay as they felt possible.

Some years ago television's 'Monty Python' team produced a sketch around a fictitious Ministry of Funny Walks. We all have a funny walk in life – just part of our strangeness – and seven of these are represented in this book: a nun, a novelist, a missionary, a journalist, an engineer, a member of parliament and a bishop.

How was this selection made? Here are two examples. The first: I unexpectedly met Sister Anna in a tiny back room of the Corrymeela Information Centre in Reading. It was a cold, grey afternoon and I was researching for some programmes on Peace and Reconciliation for Thames Television. I had seen her picture and an account of her work in a copy of *Woman's Own* with the caption: 'Sister Anna Gets On Her Bike'. There she was, adorned by a crash helmet, her face beaming at the camera as she alighted from a moped. She is a great woman. Her work in Northern Ireland supports the contention that Catholicity only means anything when there is peace to be made and reconciliation to strive for – that wholeness is an ideal only possible in a divided world, if this is any comfort.

A second example: I met Roger Hooker while researching 'The Elastic Church' for Channel 4 in 1983. He lives in Smethwick, a part of Birmingham appropriate for a section on the 'Multi-Faith' issue. It was more than interesting to meet a missionary and his wife in England who did not entirely follow the commonly understood concept of Christian mission. To those who consider the necessity of dialogue with the adherents of other faiths to be a burning issue, he has much to offer: 'Members of other faiths are not so eager for dialogue as some Christians are,' he said in the film. It is a very long road. It is so often true that traditionalists do the most *radical* things; I think of the Pope kneeling with our Primate in Canterbury. With Roger nothing is 'on show' but nothing is luke-warm either.

The conclusion to this book falls into the lap of John Taylor, who retired from the bishopric of Winchester last year. To those who consider that there is nothing but superfluity in such assemblies as the Church of England Doctrine Commission, Bishop Taylor – who has chaired the Commission – offers something like a rebuke: 'I see that as the wrong way of looking at the Church and its doctrine. As though we were a beleaguered castle, that must stay forever the same and we must defend it against attack. I see the whole thing the other way round. The Church is here for *mission* above everything else. We believe we have a story that we must tell to people, that it is relevant to all people.'

The story of Our Lord's life is unchangeable because Christians believe that it happened in reality, and so it touches all reality. But our perception of reality is not a static thing, it changes. Indeed, it must change. The ministers of the Christian story, the missionaries, are therefore faced with the duty of telling the story to people whose perceptions are in a state of flux. There must be interpretation if we are not to embed our *one life* in concrete 'for wisdom has been proved right by all her children'. The business of interpretation can go astray but we are comforted by the fact that Jesus did not ignore the plight of the lost.

John Taylor has been a missionary. We must remember that our ancestors received their faith through the agency of missionaries, not through tradition, or rather the light of mission increased in communication with the truth that exists in all surviving traditions – even my woaded forebears, for they could not have survived at all without some contact with truth; they could not have glimpsed the Christian story unless their eyes were accustomed to the light of the real.

If we have not succumbed to barbarity, or to its harbinger, narrow-mindedness, it is because some of our ancestors listened to the missionary – and if what was transmitted was real, then there must be some elements of reality surviving in this book.

TOBY CHURTON

BIOGRAPHICAL NOTES

TOBIAS CHURTON was born in 1960 in Birmingham. Educated at eight schools and at Brasenose College, Oxford, where he studied theology, he has written and directed a play *Ipsissimus* as well as five volumes of unknown poetry, including *England – The Fear of Vision.* He works chiefly as a television researcher, specializing in good religious programmes such as *The Elastic Church*, shown on Channel 4 in 1984, and *John Lennon: A Journey in the Life*, shown on BBC 1 in 1985. Having been turned down for ordination twice, he consoles himself in composing and performing music. He includes 'living' among his many interests.

SISTER ANNA is an Anglican nun, one of the Sisters of the Love of God. Sent to Belfast in 1971 under an initiative of Mother Teresa, she was named All Ireland Person of the Year in 1982 for her work criss-crossing the 'Peace Line' in the Ardoyne area of Belfast on her moped, bringing help and hope to shattered individuals and families of all beliefs and none. In 1981 she became Chairwoman of the All Children Together Movement which brought about the famous Lagan College, a pioneering initiative to create a school which integrated Protestant and Roman Catholic children. She also runs Children's Community Holidays, which serves as part of the connecting links between Lagan College and the Corrymeela Community, a community of interests, chief of which is the establishment of reconciliation and understanding between families and people of all ages who have in any way been damaged physically or mentally by 'The Troubles'. Sister Anna achieved her Master of Arts degree under the tutorship of the great Anglican theologian, Austin Farrer, in Oxford before the War.

A. N. WILSON was born in 1950. He has written a number of books, including some novels, and the biographies of John Milton and Hilaire Belloc. Now a freelance journalist, he was formerly the Literary Editor of *The Spectator*.

ROGER HOOKER was born in 1934. Educated at Charter-house and St Edmund Hall, Oxford, he was ordained in 1960. After a curacy in Stockton-on-Tees he served for thirteen years in North India under the auspices of the Church Missionary Society. For the last six of these years he was a student of the Sanskrit University, Varanasi (Banaras). He now lives in Smethwick, in the West Midlands, where his ministry is among the Asian population of the area. His main interest is in the study of Hinduism, and in the relationship between Christian faith and other faiths. He is married and has two teenage children.

NB: the opinions stated in his essay do not necessarily represent those of the Church Missionary Society.

JOHN WHALE is head of religious programmes for BBC Television. Born in December 1931, the son of the Congregationalist theologian John Seldon Whale, he read classics at Winchester and Corpus Christi College, Oxford. He has been a political and religious journalist with Independent Television News and the *Sunday Times*.

TOMMY DINGSDALE was born in May 1919 at Thatto Heath, a district of St Helens, Merseyside. He attended the local council school until he was fourteen. He went on to become a skilled engineer, an RAF Navigator and the Senior Instructor of an Engineering Training School. A Union Member of fifty-one years he was for twenty years a Works Convenor without a single day spent on strike. During fifteen years at the Training School, six hundred young people aged sixteen to seventeen gained full employment.

He was awarded the MBE in the New Year of 1984, and in March 1985 he received the distinction of being named Citizen of the Year for all Merseyside.

Retiring in September 1984, he continues to participate as Warden of St Philip's church, Derbyshire Hill; as Branch Chairman & Divisional Council Representative for the AUEW and TASS; as Executive Member of the St Helens Trades Council, and as an advisor to small businesses and Widnes Arts Council. He is also a member of the St Helens Council Training and Employment Committee.

He is married with two sons and two daughters.

FRANK FIELD has been the Member of Parliament for Birkenhead since 1979. Born in July 1942, he was educated at St Clement Danes Grammar School and Hull University. He was an Opposition spokesman on education, 1979–81, Director of the Child Poverty Action Group, 1969–79, and of the Low Pay Unit, 1974–80. Mr Field began his career as a teacher.

JOHN V. TAYLOR is one of the most respected of the Church of England's senior clerics. After a distinguished academic period at Cambridge, he was ordained priest in 1939 and served parishes in London and Lancashire before moving to the Bishop Tucker Memorial College, Mukono, Uganda in 1945. On his return to England he served the Church

Missionary Society, first as its Africa Secretary (1959–63) and then as its General Secretary (1936–74). In 1975 he became Bishop of Winchester, retiring to Oxford in 1985.

Sister Anna

Sister Anna

I WAS BROUGHT UP, as were my parents, an Anglican. This was not, however, without questioning. By the time I was confirmed, I was well aware of other Christian Churches and shocked those preparing me by remarking: 'Just because I'm Anglican born, does not mean I should remain one.'

God found me when I was five. I had ignored him until then. When one comes face to face with God, it is self-evident that one belongs to him totally, body, mind and spirit, and then one desires only him. So I knew at once, in embryonic form, without of course understanding it, that I would be radically poor and would not marry. I knew nothing yet of positive celibacy; but all this was already in the realm of desire, not of law: not a binding, but a freeing. This has led me, through many ordinary and extraordinary experiences, to the vocation, accepted and blessed by the Church, of a monastic pilgrim: very simply seeking to live a life of prayer on the roads of the world, serving my neighbour, depending on Providence for guidance and all support. God has always been very real and present to me: not as a unitary monad, but One in Three Persons, each of whom we experience in a subtly different way.

I belong to a Community: The Sisters of the Love of God, without which my life would be untenable and unimaginable. Here I am deep-rooted. Here I owe obedience, returning home from time to time and going out again, spiritually replenished, as Providence directs. In such a Community, whose work is prayer, everything is discarded which does not help towards constant awareness of the presence of God, every activity is turned into prayer: it is a way of life in which silence and enclosure are loved and cherished. The Community does not support me materially when I am not there, understanding that I need to live without this. It is no problem for the Lord of all things to keep one little person nourished and clothed.

This means that I have knocked about the world through three continents. Not only have I lived with Anglicans in the Church of England, the Church of Ireland, the Church in Wales, the Episcopal Churches of Scotland and of the USA. I have also lived with Lutherans, Reformed, Orthodox, Roman Catholic and other Christians – lived for many years, that is, not just looked at them from the outside: lived intensely, following their pattern of spiritual life.

Despite having lived for long periods with other Christian Churches, I seem more deeply rooted in Anglicanism than ever. Why do I give profound and unreserved thanks for being an Anglican, while still appreciating the riches of others?

I was listening recently to Bishop Desmond Tutu on the BBC, describing what it means in practice for the Churches, suffering in one part of the world, to be upheld by the prayers of the Church universal in some remote spot elsewhere. This experience of living as part of the one Body is central to Anglicanism.

To me, the universal Church is the most inspiring fact in the world. This reality transcends time and space, it transcends history. Like an iceberg, only the tip is visible here and now. The greater part is already beyond space and time, alive in Christ and interacting with us, strengthening us.

The work of Christ and the fruits of the Spirit are miraculous. One is redeemed out of the fallen world's disintegration into at-one-ment, incorporated into the one Body of Christ which, by his action, overcomes all human divisions without exception. I see the work of the devil as essentially to estrange and separate: to bring personal disintegration, family division, the tearing apart of races, classes, nations: Babel, in fact, rooted in pride and arrogance. When the values and spirit of worldliness have invaded and weakened the Churches, they compromise with the divisions of the world, become part of one side or the other, more or less blocking the power of Christ to heal. They become unaware that they are radically different, called to cut right across boundaries and be freed from racism, tribalism, nationalism, imperialism and all other human -isms.

So to me the Church is also the most depressing institution in the world, humanly regarded. How abysmally we fail to live out this reality. What a pathetically pale and distorted reflection of this oneness we present to the world. We do not allow Christ to overcome either the world's disunities, or our own internal ones. How small-minded, how exclusive we are! Yet evil never has the last word. We are ever being called to repentance and greater fidelity. The Lord is always knocking at the door.

Already, before becoming a pilgrim, when training as a teacher, I chose as the theme for my college lecture 'The contribution of the Churches to the Church Universal' and prepared for this talk by seeking to live with and get alongside Christians of other traditions.

I then studied theology at Oxford, where we would go to a Baptist Hebraic scholar for parts of the Old Testament, to Dominicans for Patristic studies: to the experts, regardless of denomination. My tutor was Austin Farrer, a person of extraordinary intellectual selflessness, with a kind of chastity of spirit, always utterly humble before truth, never 'possessing' it. There was never a sense of master and pupil. It was just one vast exploration together. How congruous it seemed, of a summer evening, to be sitting in an ancient window, overlooking the college gardens, immersed in the early Fathers!

There I also came into the orbit of two great confessors of the Faith: Fr Somerset Ward and Fr Gilbert Shaw. I began to experience some of the many strands of spirituality, which, in a marvellous way, have been preserved in the Anglican tradition; but it requires the guidance of the Holy Spirit to discover them.

It was also during this time that I had an experience which turned me inside out. Up until then I had been an activist: living for God, using all I had in his service. Quite suddenly, out of the blue, I was confronted with the fact of the Religious Life, of this element within the life of the Church that I had previously ignored. That God should call some people, simply in the freedom of his will, to *be* for him, not necessarily to engage in any activity, but just to depend upon him for everything, to find everything in him, to exist for his good pleasure, amazed me and plucked me up from the earth, as it were, into a state of suspension. It is a vocation, a state of life, in which God alone matters and one's external circumstances are supremely unimportant: one can be as serene in activity or in a crowd as in solitude or terminal illness. The one thing is to seek to live constantly in the beam of his will, which he makes known by external circumstance and inner pressures. Just as it was rediscovered in the Anglican Church in the last century, the Religious Life is in this century steadily making its way

into the Churches of the Reformation and more and more
Communities are springing up. Yet it is open to everyone
living a 'normal' life to live in such a way that everything
becomes response and dependence, not self-initiated, not
non-activity, but activity-within-passivity, although it can
never be completely learned in this life.

It is strange that even in predominantly Catholic countries, such as France, in my wanderings I always seemed
to be thrown together with Orthodox. I never made a
deliberate choice. I was for over five years in the only free
Orthodox country – Greece – and could hardly get away.
I lived in Orthodox Communities, Greek, Russian, Serbian
and Arabic, and so became familiar with that rich liturgical
tradition in Greek and Old Slavonic. In those days, had I
been a Protestant, I would hardly have been acceptable;
had I been a Roman Catholic, I would hardly have been
permitted. Now things are more flexible.

I love Orthodoxy. It is essentially a corporately praying
Church with its inspired hymnology, theologically sound
and perceptive, poetically right. I recall the deep respect
paid to the mother of the Saviour, yet she is never depicted
in an icon without her Son and is never placed above him
in a group of icons. I hear the paradoxes of the Christmas
office: 'He whom the heaven of heavens cannot contain,
wrapped in swaddling bands. He who nourishes all creation, nourished by his mother's milk . . .' I see, at the
beginning of Lent, each member of a Community begging
forgiveness of the others with a prostration, and the whole
Community prostrate, after each of the seven daily services,
begging 'to see my own sins and not those of my brother'.
What a difference it makes to the Community life! We in
the West have not been vouchsafed the gift of rich and
profound hymnology. Yet I do not believe the Orthodox
have been given it to hug to themselves and indeed many

western Communities have now developed liturgies with a strongly Orthodox flavour. One does, however, acknowledge and love the particular tradition of liturgy preserved in the whole monastic life of the West, condensed in Anglican matins and evensong, experienced at its most inspiring in our great cathedrals.

I am an Anglican fundamentally because I believe we are in the Truth (as I believe Orthodoxy to be organically part of the true stream of the Church Universal). There is nothing whatsoever unacceptable to me in either tradition, although the Orthodox are more clear cut, Anglicans more inclusive. God called me to be an Anglican and he has never called me to be anything else.

I have found the sense of the Church to be the same in Orthodoxy and Anglicanism. For both, the Body of Christ is organic, united through time and space from apostolic times by the bishops, who hold it together in a living unity, like the frame of a body, yet personal and spiritual, for bishops are persons, set aside sacramentally by the action of the Holy Spirit. It was essential for the English Reformers to preserve our oneness with the universal Church from earliest times by retaining the episcopate (among other things), realizing that one cannot re-found the Church. This would be a contradiction of its very nature: 'We believe in one holy, catholic (universal) and apostolic Church', founded by Christ, as an aspect of redemption. Because indwelt by the Spirit, however corrupt, it never disintegrates into non-existence, for through repentance comes renewal. I am glad that, because of this continuity, we have no special Anglican doctrines. We hold the faith of the undivided Church, laid down by the ecumenical councils of the first seven centuries, even though there are times when we have been confused as to what this faith is. This credo cannot be added to while the Church is in schism. Doctrinal formulas are only external 'counters' as it were, but they express realities which are beyond expression. This was borne in upon me vividly in Greece, where my closest friend is someone of a very different background. She was married at fifteen, illiterate when we met, lived in a house with a mud floor and no water or electricity. Before we ever had a common language, which came gradually, we experienced in practice the *identity* of faith. We were living the same great realities, transcending denomination, intellect, even speech. These truths are not ideas, but facts: practical, spiritual ones.

I am often asked when I am abroad whether I am a 'low' Anglican, 'high', or 'central'. Abhorring little boxes, I reply that I'm just Anglican. The strength and purity of the 'evangelical' element and the stress on the need for total personal surrender to and dependence on Jesus is vital and who among us is fully so? Yet it can remain individualistic and stunted if it does not flower into the total corporate experience of the Body, into which we are growing all the time, making one discovery after another as we seek to live the Christian life. I have seen this flowering in a number of people. I am happy with both ends of the spectrum, but happier still with the fruitful interaction between them. In the words of Amand de Amendieta: 'The fullness of Anglicanism will be utterly catholic and uncompromisingly evangelical at the same time, all of the same breath.'

In the West these two elements fell apart and we are only gradually rediscovering the integrity of the faith. In some ways, the whole Anglican community is a microcosm of the terrible lack of unity in the Church at large. There are very bitter divisions of all kinds among Anglicans: there are parties, divisions, dissensions right in the middle of the search for unity of spirit. Penitence and prayer here are absolutely vital, not only for Anglicanism, but for the

Church as a whole. 'We are members of one another. If one member flourishes, we all flourish together,' as St Paul says.

Throughout history the Eastern Church has been subjected far more to external attack than to aberrations within. What a joy it is to find here a wholeness of catholic tradition with a very evangelical spirit, as well as a sense of the wholeness of body, mind and spirit. Coming West, Eastern Christians have been amazed at the rationalism in both Reformed and Counter-reformed traditions, rationalism in every sphere, both doctrinal and disciplinary. Maybe the national weakness of the pragmatic English, who prefer to 'muddle through', has to some extent preserved the Anglican Communion (which stemmed from the English Church, both Celtic and Latin at root) from this widespread impoverishment and deformation.

I believe – and here I am particularly influenced by Eastern Orthodox teaching – that spiritual freedom is the crown of the spiritual life. As St Paul said and Luther after him, freedom in the Spirit has nothing to do with laxity, for it 'costs not less than everything' in Eliot's phrase.

'Why are you not Orthodox?' people say. Why should I be? Unless they live in certain centres, Western Orthodox have a terrible time, deprived of church and sacraments. As an Anglican, I have been immensely nourished, strengthened, led on, never repressed or coerced. Here I have found everything and freedom to expand in Christ; nor have I ever met with any arbitrary 'external' authority. Obedience is, as it were, the backbone of the Religious Life; but there is nothing small in my Superior, only a very pure and burning love of God and of his will, which enables us to discern it together, even when this leads to surprising and unexpected conclusions. There has been nothing non-personal in my experience of religious obedience. It has been more a question of transparency, of seeking to be totally open, and then consensus in perceiving what God wants. When I was for a longer period in a Russian Community, I had in fact, two Superiors: the Russian Abbess for daily living and my own Superior back home for major decisions; but that presented no conflict, no problem either.

From the above, it is perhaps clear that although nourished by Scripture, I live in the whole great tradition and do not look primarily to the Reformation. I am not completely at home in any Protestant Church. Yet how we need each other! The churches in France have discovered this: 'We belong together,' they say. Many Catholics revere their Reformed brethren: the current of evangelical purity, the 'exclamation mark in the margin' as Barth said. Certainly Reformed Christians realize there that they could not exist without the Catholic Church.

The Church of Rome has recently passed through a Reformation, not wholly unlike that of the sixteenth century, and the evangelical, simple, spiritual side shines out with renewed brightness. I have known Roman Catholic Christians second to none in their luminosity; but I have also experienced time and again the frustrations of colleagues of that communion who, wholly committed to seeking to live in and by Christ, sailing ahead in a free and 'evangelical' way, have then suddenly been pulled up short by 'authority' and sometimes put out of action altogether. I suppose one of the reasons why I am not a Roman Catholic is because of their attitude to control; I see a certain fear, leading to legalism and an overweight of bureaucracy; a certain lack of faith in the ability of the Holy Spirit to keep the Church on course.

Although many Roman Catholics would not now hold that their Church is *the* Church, to which all others must be gathered in, yet there is still an ambiguity here. Communion with the Bishop of Rome is still seen by many to be the factor that constitutes the unity of the Church. Unless the Church of Rome is *the* Church, how can new dogmas be promulgated unilaterally from Rome? Personally I would be quite happy to recognize the Pope as our western patriarch 'inter pares', united in sacramental equality with all the other bishops and patriarchs, but I cannot accept the papacy as another order altogether. It is to me a centralization which has an administrative rather than a sacramental basis, in that there is no *sacramental* order above bishops.

It is ultimately a question of faith. One either believes it, or one does not. Truth and charity lie very close together. To my mind, uncharitable, bitter, polemical attacks on the papacy led inevitably to over-emphasis upon it.

I believe the whole Church to be in schism: the eleventh-century Great Schism between East and West, the fragmentations of the Reformation and later divisions, have split the Church apart. The Anglican Church is in schism. We certainly are in no position to promulgate dogmas of the Church unilaterally.

I have always had a firm belief that, however much our little Anglican boat may stray off course, or lean over out of the true (and God knows our infidelities, muddled thinking and incomprehensions), the Holy Spirit can be relied upon to bring us back on centre in his own good time. Modernisms become out of date and fade away. I am glad that our theological system prefers weakness to legalism, even though this puts a strain on our clergy which not all of them can carry.

People seem surprised when I say: 'I would not wish to unsettle anyone in their faith.' I do *not* believe in proselytism. It is the work of the Spirit within to lead people on to where they should be going; no good comes of our clumsy well-intentioned shoving from without.

As I see it, the Church is like a garden full of blooms, presenting altogether a riot of colour, not meant to be separated off behind little fences. The gradual unifying, co-inherence and flowing into one another will come in God's own way and time, as we cease to be afraid of one another, to put up barriers, to wish to dominate. Unity in his will is his work, to which we must be attentive and responsive. I do not believe in the flowers being pulled up by the roots and planted elsewhere, unless the inner compulsion is almost irresistible. I have at least two friends who are Anglican-Quakers. It combines well. I have no inner compulsion to move and never have had.

Thirteen years ago, when I happened to be in my Community, Mother Teresa of Calcutta met our Warden and asked him to find four 'protestant nuns' to join her four Sisters in Belfast. This was one of the times I was drawn out again by Providence for I was asked if I would go. After a year, the other seven were needed elsewhere and withdrawn. I stayed on as a kind of freelance worker for reconciliation. The last thing I am here is a parish worker, within narrow confines. I am not tied by family obligations or a nine to five job. I am free to respond to those little shoots of new life which are springing up everywhere in Northern Ireland, as a result, I believe, of faithful prayer from all over the world which is watering the hard ground. I am not an idealist. I abhor planting ideas on other people for them to carry out. I believe my role to be like a midwife or gardener, not able to create life, but only to minister to what is emerging by the Creator's act. It is an inspiration to be here because so much is happening. The media tend to present a picture of endless hatred, bitterness and violence. From the ground, the picture is quite different and incomparably more helpful – so may believing people not grow weary in praying!

The first thing that struck us in Northern Ireland was that everything was '*us and them*'. Society had fallen apart. There was little sense of the common good. On the whole, with notable exceptions, the Churches are still enmeshed in this tribal division: they are part of the problem. They have for too long been 'representing our people' in the sense of our tribe, rather than primarily being conscious that we are citizens of another Kingdom, into which we are freed as a new creation: freed from fear, freed from bondage to our history and to over-identification with our tribe.

People here say, 'I was with some Protestants today' or 'some Catholics'. I do not notice, being with people all day long, right across the spectrum, mixing all the time. Unexpectedly, instead of finding barriers at the beginning, because I was English, I was given greater freedom than if I had been solidly embedded in a tribe, yet fraternizing with 'them uns'. People here are so warm-hearted, hospitable and genuine that it is easy to reach the real person inside a sectarian crust. Obviously, the people I find myself closest to are not either 'them' or 'us', but committed Christians, believing folk who are seeking to live out their fidelity to Jesus in the service of others, regardless of sectarian divisions, and there are many, many, such people, deeply involved in the community as a whole.

Nevertheless, as an Anglican in Northern Ireland, I am keenly aware of being descended from that church which was established by law and which persecuted Roman Catholic and Presbyterian alike – the penal laws, for instance, continued in Ireland much longer than in Britain. Those of us who are English and Anglican have to acknowledge responsibility for much of the hideous past of suffering in

Ireland, as well as the seemingly intractable tangles of the present. An Anglican therefore must always be seeking forgiveness and making amends in whatever way possible.

At the same time it is true that the Church of Ireland has a role as a *bridge church*. To Roman Catholics we are simply Protestants. To many Presbyterians we are Papists to all intents and purposes. Clearly this can be turned to positive and constructive ends. As reformed Catholics, even if a scandal to both, we yet have sympathies and at least a degree of understanding in both directions. We are children of the Reformation, with its cry of *sola gratia:* by God's pure gift alone is the whole cosmos redeemed. Nevertheless the Anglican Church was not a sixteenth-century creation and, as already stated, our continuity with the universal Church from the beginning is of prime importance to us.

It is possible, however, that the Church of Ireland has first to discover its full self: its own identity. Because of its peculiar history, it is not altogether representative of the Anglican spirit. Maybe it has to discover, unafraid and more strongly, its links with the full catholic tradition, in order to regain its true balance.

Berdyaev often said that most of us just absorb the prevailing outlook. In the Middle Ages, those who were thus 'cabbages' were believers. Only original thinkers were atheist or agnostic. Today in Western Europe it is the other way round. Cabbages are now atheist, original thinkers Christian. We live in a society which ignores God in practice, whatever the lip service. To most people therefore all the foregoing is simply non-sense, meaningless; but in any case, to become a believer is a gift from above: 'Except a man be born of water and of the Spirit, he cannot enter into the kingdom of God.' If it is impossible to flesh and blood to believe in God, how much more of a miracle is required to perceive the Church, especially our Anglican

Church, as the Body of Christ. How can anyone, seeing only our infidelities, understand us from without? We present such an odd picture in our poverty and weakness; but it is not what we are that is at fault, but how we live it out: to an Anglican, a constant challenge. We *are* nourished by the life of God, but it needs eyes to see.

I am convinced we cannot float about individualistically; we must be rooted somewhere in the Church; nor do I believe we can create a 'Church of Unity', which becomes yet another schism.

To me certainly the disunity of the Church is the ultimate infidelity, blasphemous, sacrilegious, profaning the Body, man-made, artificial, marring the new creation into which Jesus has redeemed us. This division is rooted in pride and arrogance. We proclaim at-one-ment in Christ. We live the opposite. We have inherited this. We cannot get out of it by our own efforts. But we *can* press forward into the unity into which our Lord is calling us all by penitence, believing and unwearied prayer and hard work. We can and must; since this unity is somehow *there* all the time. If it were not, we could not find it. To enter into this requires for us all a fearless, open, attentive and inclusive attitude to all that is of him, from whatever quarter it comes. Yet it is sure. It is the living reality of life in Christ, a gift of God.

A. N. Wilson

A. N. Wilson

EVERY FEW MILES, dotted all over England, there are churches. Some of them are new; some of them have been there for hundreds of years. Most contain some sort of beauty; all of them have been visited by men and women because they wanted to worship God, or merely to confront the mystery of their own existence on this mysterious earth. Many non-Christian or half-Christian people value these buildings, and the value they place on them is different in kind from the value attaching to other old buildings such as stately homes or ruined castles. Even if we can no longer pray, these buildings are monuments of prayer: monuments, not tombs, and, as a Christian believer would say, living stones which represent the spiritual aspirations not just of individuals, but of the whole human race crying out to God as Father.

That cry, *Our Father*, and the prayer which follows it, is sometimes painted up on the board at the eastern end of our parish churches. Usually the words are to be found over the holy table, or whatever you call that object of furniture. In some churches it can look like a gloriously decked altar with rich stuff hanging in front of it, and lit with candles; or it can be a plain table, very recognizably 'God's board' at which the people come to be fed. As most visitors to a church will know, it is from this table that the sacrament of Holy Communion is distributed. In some churches, to mark the extreme solemnity with which

33

Christians regard this sacrament, the table is hidden behind rails and screens. They remind us of the distance between men and God; and like the opening phrases of the Lord's prayer, they remind us of his holiness and otherness. In other churches, the holy table stands in the midst of the seats and pews, expressing another truth, that God is with us, and that he came into this world to save us sinners.

Most visitors to the church would have a vague sense of this symbolism. Inevitably, it leaves most people cold, as they turn towards the door and wonder whether to sign the book ('Lovely atmosphere') or even to put money in the wall box ('Church expenses' for the middle stumpers; 'candles' for the high; 'holy souls' if you are going through the roof).

There is another thing by the door. It is the font and during the eighteenth century fonts were often kept in the parson's garden and used as bird baths. In Victorian times they were moved back into the church, for their true function is not for sparrows to paddle in, nor even to grow parsley, but for baptism. This is not a mere naming ceremony. It is the sacrament which initiates our collective life in Christ, or to put it another way, it is the sacrament which admits us to membership of the Church. In baptism, St Paul thought, we enter into the mystery of Christ's death and rise with him in glory.

Pause by the font and ask yourself: Is there a God or isn't there? If there is, did he create the world and then leave it to get on with its own sorry history? Or did he, as the Bible teaches, love the world and watch its progress? Is he the sort of God who can only reveal himself to very holy people in sudden mystic flashes? Or is he, as Christians believe, the God of all the human race and all creation, who chose to enter his creation, and be human and live among us?

It is the belief of Christians that the Lord's prayer, and baptism and the Lord's Supper were all given to the world by God himself as tokens of his presence. The old craftsmen who painted the words *Our Father* over the holy table did not do so because they thought the words were inspiring, or because they got a lump in their throats thinking of how their mothers taught them the prayer. They painted up the words because they believed that God himself had said them; that God himself had taught us that in these words we could communicate with him. Similarly, they did not carve beautiful fonts because they thought there was an attractive symbolism in pouring water over a child's head. They believed that there really *is* such a thing as evil and that when we pour that water over someone's head we free them from servitude to evil, and place them in the service of God, which is perfect freedom. Similarly, the many ways in which architects and church furnishers have decked and displayed Christian altars and holy tables reflect the fact that the eucharist is at the centre of Christian worship. Christians believe that it was instituted by Christ himself 'in the same night that he was betrayed', and that he commanded his followers to 'do this in remembrance of me'. That, in fact, is why there are churches at all: to house the eucharist.

There is strong evidence that these three things – the *Our Father*, baptism, and eucharist stretch back to the beginning of Christendom. Anyone who feels the compulsion to be a Christian, anyone caught up in that strange adventure, must return to this central fact. And if one had to answer the question, '*Why do you still go to church?*' the answer must be, 'To receive Holy Communion.' This is the sacrament which sustains and nourishes the Christian. He comes to it knowing that he comes to the physician of life who, in the words of the old prayer, 'will heal his sickness, wash his foulness, enlighten his blindness, enrich his poverty and clothe his nakedness' through this act. But, equally, one does not receive the sacrament merely for 'religious uplift'. Christians go up to the altar rails because they believe they should. 'Do this in remembrance of me.'

This decision, that there really is a God, and that he revealed himself in Jesus Christ and that he feeds us in the sacraments of Jesus Christ is the greatest thing in life. But of course it cannot be taken in a vacuum. And it brings us down to earth with a bit of a bang to recognize that these sacraments are dispensed by the Reverend Mr Blank or (heaven save us) Bishop So-and-so. Is there no other way of following the commandments of Christ than by becoming involved in this set-up, which so often forcibly reminds us of the army officer during the First World War who, on being asked his impression of the trenches exclaimed, 'My dear, the *noise* and the *people!*'

Certainly there would not be many communicants at the altar rails next Sunday if by kneeling they were obliged to endorse much of what is going on in the Church of England at the present time. If we judged the Church solely by the public pronouncements of its more foolish bishops, or by the crazier resolutions of the General Synod, we would find ourselves fast disillusioned (or I hope we should).

But what if there came a point where the 'people' were not merely uncongenial but unChristian? What if the noise became not merely disgusting, but profane? For instance, there are obviously many people in senior positions in the Church of England who do not believe that Christianity is a revealed religion in the sense that I have defined it in the earlier paragraphs of this essay. They believe, evidently, that the rules and the ordinances of the Church, and the creeds, and the New Testament itself are of purely human origin. They believe that the sacraments of the Church were

evolved through purely human means to meet particular
religious needs at particular junctures of history. They do
not believe that Jesus Christ was the incarnate Son of God,
who came to earth and told us to use the Lord's prayer, or
to baptize all nations. They do not believe that God raised
Jesus Christ from the dead in the way the Bible says he
did. Still less do they believe that Jesus was the pre-existent
Son of God, begotten by his Father 'before all worlds'.
They therefore see no reason to believe that he was born
without the agency of a human father.

Does the widespread existence of unbelief on this scale
threaten to drive out those who believe in the 'faith once
delivered to the saints'? Evidently many individuals have
found that it did, and they have scuttled off for safety to
the intellectually obscurantist Orthodox or to the rigorists
whom they believe to be most representative of Rome.
But there is an element, very often, of unChristian fear in
such a flight; and more than an element of seeing a mote
of doubt in someone else's eye in order to hide from oneself
the beam of doubt in one's own. The Church of England
never has disputed the creeds, the Bible, and so on. In fact,
even the General Synod has repeatedly asserted its belief in
them. But the deliberations of that body, thank God, do
not concern the religious life of anyone in England. It is a
self-regarding, extravagant irrelevance.

Why, in spite of all the muddle and the annoyance and
the sheer tenth-rateness of the modern Church, why do I
continue to go?

First, I am glad to belong to the Church of England
because it is the Church of *England*. It is the Church to
which the majority of my fellow countrymen notionally
belong, and to which the great majority of English Christians in the past in fact belonged. I think of all the griefs
and wisdom of Samuel Johnson; I think of Jane Austen and

Tennyson growing up in their fathers' parsonage houses; I think of the heroic slum priests of Victorian London, such as Alexander Heriot Mackonochie or Charles Lowder; I think of all the poets from George Herbert to T. S. Eliot; I think of learned and holy men like Darwell Stone; I think of holy simpletons like Lilian Bayliss, the founder of the Old Vic; I think of rustic congregations listening to the sermons of the Reverend Francis Kilvert; I think of Whig duchesses hooting with mirth at the dinner conversation of the Reverend Sidney Smith; I think of the urban poor in places like St Alban's, Holborn or St Peter's, London Docks; I think of attractive technicoloured religious nutters such as Father Ignatius of Llanthony; I think of figures as different as Rose Macaulay and C. S. Lewis; Barbara Pym and John Betjeman; Mother Millicent Taylor and King George V. They all, more or less, lived within the fold of the Church of England, and they all died within it. If I left the Church of England I would feel I was leaving them.

So much for the people. Now the noise. I am glad to belong to a church with a magnificent musical and choral tradition and a liturgy, still used in some places, which is incomparably euphonious, endlessly repeatable. Recently I decided that I should not get stuck in my ways so I started to read the psalms in the modern Roman Catholic version. Within three weeks I was happily back with Coverdale. I am told that one of the most popular services on the radio is Choral Evensong. It was so popular that instead of it being once, they now broadcast it twice a week.

Thirdly, I love the buildings of the Church of England. Nothing wrong with that. It is something more than mere aestheticism. I could echo Betjeman's lines:

still for me
The steps to truth were made by sculptured stone,
Stained glass and vestments, holy water stoups,
Incense and crossings of myself – the things
That hearty middle stumpers most despise
As 'all the inessentials of the faith'.

There is also the special sort of pleasure associated with an old thing still in use. How bleak an old house feels when no one lives there and all its furniture, china, glass and silver are merely museum pieces for the National Trust. If you wander through an old house that is still inhabited, you will find spectacles and a detective novel next to the bed 'used by Charles I' or crumbs on the ormolu sideboard. Some lucky people still live there and use these things for the purposes they were meant for. And Anglicans are the lucky people who still stand in the choir stalls of our old cathedrals, or preach wonderfully stodgy sermons from eighteenth-century wine-glass pulpits. They are using their old buildings (when the Church Commissioners and the bishops allow them) for the purposes for which they were made.

Fourthly, I believe that there are signs of God's grace working in the Church, even now. God is 'within no walls confined', and I don't believe he is the possession of any one Church, nor even of Christians alone. He is God. He is too big for that. But my myopic half-glimpses have come most frequently in an Anglican setting. I think of a priest who, without any show or fuss, quite simply worked miracles of healing. (Dead now.) I think of the witness of prayer given by our religious communities. I think of the shrine of Our Lady of Walsingham. I think of some of the lives that have touched my own, the lives of people who are or were much better Christians than I am, and who were able, within the Church of England, to enter into Christ's work of reconciling the world to himself. If the Church of England is good enough for them, it is good enough for a sinner like me.

Fifthly, I return to where I began, to the sacramental life. I do not find it easy to be a Christian. My character is lamentably out of tune with the ideals of perfection set out in the Sermon on the Mount. As much as anyone living in this juncture of the twentieth century, I am separated from a pure vision of God by thick clouds of sin, doubt, muddle. But if God *was* in Christ, reconciling the world to himself, I have no chance of apprehending his treasures, nor of entering into his mystery, nor of being touched by his love, if I am disloyal to my understanding of what he said. I do not believe that he condemns those who understand him differently. But for me, *Do this in remembrance of me* is an inescapable command. 'We are not worthy so much as to gather up the crumbs under thy table, but thou art the same Lord, whose property is always to have mercy.' It is to him that one turns and not to 'the Church' and still less to the bishops and the Synod, or the *Church Times*, as one leaves one's pew and very hesitantly goes up to the altar rails.

Roger Hooker

Roger Hooker

I WAS BROUGHT UP to belong to the Church of England. It provided the setting in which Christian faith first became real to me, and the language in which it found expression. Above all, it offered, and continues to offer, a style and an atmosphere which correspond more closely to my felt needs than any other pattern of Christianity which I have so far encountered. At the heart of the Anglican way there is the great principle of restraint. We Anglicans do not wear our hearts on our sleeves, nor do we believe in self-advertisement. Like great music or great poetry Anglicanism has to be pondered, lived with, and explored. One grows into it. What Anglicans believe is not, for the most part, different from what Christians of every time and place have believed. What does distinguish us from others is the way in which those beliefs are held.

Ours is only one possible way of being Christian, and therefore we need both to see it and to live it in conscious relationship with other ways. To do this is to realize that its strengths are also its limitations. An example from literature can make the point: Jane Austen always strikes me as being a characteristically Anglican writer. Her novels are based on that principle of restraint; what she and her characters leave unsaid is often more important than what they actually put into words. Yet to turn from her to Dostoievsky or Kazantzakis is to realize that there are heights and depths of human experience that she never plumbed. In the same way, to be an Anglican is implicitly to realize that we are only a minority of the world Church. We have an important and distinctive contribution to make both to world-wide Christianity and to the life of our own country, but we can only presume to offer it if we first recognize that the very different contributions of other Churches are as important and certainly no less distinctive than our own.

To put that in more directly personal terms: the Church of England is my spiritual home. Here I can truly be myself in the presence of God, and find vision, forgiveness, renewal, and a particularly precious kind of companionship on the Christian way. Yet it is a commonplace to say that we only really discover our home when we have left it. 'He knows not England who only England knows.' The converse is also true. My experience has continually taken me across frontiers into unfamiliar worlds – of other forms of Christianity and, even more, of other religions, cultures and languages. To explore the unfamiliar I need to know where I belong. Without the security of home one cannot be an explorer, but only a refugee. One reason why I am still an Anglican today is that this tradition continues to give me both the security which makes exploring possible and the freedom which encourages me to undertake it.

The proper balance between freedom and security depends on another important Anglican principle, that of dispersed authority. There is no one place in our common life where final authority is to be located. We look to Scripture, to tradition and to reason; to bishops, synods and the individual conscience. Yet we have never allowed any one of these to dominate and overrule the others. This means that there is a certain lack of definition in what we believe. This allows for diversity which is wholly good, but it also means that we have sometimes found it impossible to make up our collective mind, not least in union negotiations with other churches. Embarrassment to ourselves and great hurt to others have been the result, indeed we have to ask ourselves today whether we have a collective mind at all. Are we anything more than an uneasy alliance of different groups of Christians held together by a historic link with the state? Could the Church of England survive dis-establishment? Both the content of Anglican doctrine and its boundaries need to be more sharply delineated.

I find that therefore I have to be a critical Anglican, but the perspective from which I make my criticism is largely governed by my past experience. I must therefore offer some account of it.

My early years were very little different from those of many others of my background and generation. My parents were devout Anglicans and that was the way they brought us up. Among my earliest memories are the prayers they taught me to say at night. In later years I was much impressed by the way my prep school headmaster took prayers, and later still our vicar, Henry de Candole, had a similar if more profound effect. Both men took a keen personal interest in me. It is to them and to my home that I trace the roots of my faith.

At this stage my Anglicanism was wholly unselfcon-scious and when the headmaster of my public school, knowing I was an ordinand, asked me if I was Catholic or Evangelical, I could only reply that I didn't know. Up till then I had never heard of either term. This deficiency in my knowledge was remedied when I was sixteen. I was invited to go to a 'camp' for public school boys. Here for the first time I encountered the evangelical tradition in the shape of group Bible study, extempore prayer, and a relaxed and informal atmosphere. I also found the joy that lies at the heart of authentic Christianity, I discovered that Christ had died for me personally and that I must consciously decide for him.

All this I eagerly embraced for it seemed to me to be what I had been obscurely searching after. More than that, I found a warmth of fellowship and emotional security at a time when my mother's long illness had made life at home something of an ordeal. But in the end I found that I could not stomach the literalist interpretation of the Bible and the authoritarian style of leadership which went with it. So after national service and during my second year at Oxford I took a painful leave of the camps and the Inter-Collegiate Christian Union to which I had also belonged. I owed them a great debt, even though I could no longer see Christian discipleship that way.

In 1958 I went to Wycliffe Hall, also in Oxford, to train for ordination. Here I was part of a community which lived, worshipped, studied and explored together. I loved it all, and at last had found a context in which mind and spirit could put down roots and grow. It was a characteristically Anglican context, though I did not fully realize this at the time.

Looking back, it all seems very tame and circumscribed, for these were the days before jeans, long hair and *Honest to God* – the visible symbols of the massive social and intellectual earthquake which began in the sixties.

I did not experience this earthquake for at the end of my first year at Wycliffe Hall I spent a week in bed with flu. While I was recovering I read Constance Padwick's biography of Temple Gairdner. This beautifully written and sensitive portrait of a great Anglican was to set my life on a new course. Gairdner had spent himself as a missionary in Cairo, but he was a very different kind of person from the caricature which the word 'missionary' often suggests. When I had fully recovered I read Kenneth Cragg's *The*

Call of the Minaret – a book which not only offered a sympathetic and scholarly account of Islam, but also helped me to make much more sense of Christianity by setting it in a new context. It was only when I began to grasp the Islamic view of divine revelation – which was uncomfortably close to the kind of Christianity which I had so recently rejected – that the incarnation started to become intelligible.

I had just won a distinction in the Oxford Diploma in Theology, and now I knew that I had to dedicate my intellectual powers, such as they were, to the exploration of other religions. I had to find ways of confessing the Christ within in ways which not only did justice to my own faith, but also to all that was good and positive in the faith of others.

So it was that in 1965 I found myself in India, under the auspices of the Church Missionary Society. By now I was married and my wife and I devoted our first two years to the study of Hindi, the *lingua franca* of much of North India. At the language school we lived and studied with over a hundred and fifty people from many different countries and Christian denominations. Both as English and as Anglicans we were in a minority – a new and salutary experience. It was also enriching, for now we were able to discover at first hand what we had always known, that as Christians we belonged to a world-wide company whose unity was deeper than any distinctions of race, colour, culture and language. At the same time I became more self-conscious in my Anglicanism and more deeply convinced that this was the way for me.

But my explorations were to take me into much more unfamiliar territory than this. For three and a half years I taught in the Hindi language at a theological college for Indian Christian pastors who were to serve in the villages of North India. Their mental and spiritual world was totally different from my own. For one thing, life for them was essentially corporate. The language had no word for 'privacy', the nearest equivalent meaning was 'loneliness'. The whole notion of sitting down by oneself and reading a book was unfamiliar to them. Many of them had experienced their Christian vocation through a dream. To try to turn such men into Anglicans was to clothe them in Goliath's armour, never mind Saul's. I began to realize how heavily my own tradition depends on words. All too easily we ignore other dimensions of experience. Worse still, we unconsciously disenfranchise those who do not know our pattern of words. Language is power.

This conviction grew deeper as I studied and experienced Hinduism, with its round of festival, pilgrimage, fast and feast, and with its deep roots in the land. Here was a form of religion in which the right words were much less important, and which seemed more akin to the Catholicism of Southern Europe than anything I had encountered hitherto. I also discovered the philosophical side of the Hindu tradition when for six years I was the only Christian student at the Sanskrit University of Varanasi (Banaras). Here, by contrast, words were very important and were used with a razor-sharp precision.

I found within Hinduism much to respect and admire, some things which challenged me, others which perhaps baffled or repelled. Above all I got to know Hindus who offered me their friendship. To discover another religious tradition through the eyes of those who live within it is very different from seeing it in a purely academic context.

Yet at the same time all that I discovered enabled me to see my own faith in new ways. I became more deeply impressed by the distinctiveness of Jesus and of that personal love of God which Christians see supremely focused in Jesus Christ. Further, my absence from England somehow helped me to discover much within the Anglican tradition. Now for the first time I read Herbert, Traherne and many other writers.

We returned to Britain in 1978 and now live in the West Midlands where I have a responsibility for ministry among people of Asian origin within an Anglican inner city deanery. I have to ask myself what, if anything, the Church of England can offer people living in an area such as this which is racially mixed and culturally fragmented. That question has a more than merely local or personal significance, for in some respects Britain's inner city areas today are a microcosm of the wider world.

My years in India, and return visits made since I left, convince me that irreversible changes have now taken place in our common life. Modern technology, especially in the field of communications, means that ideas and information can now travel very quickly to almost everywhere on earth. Air travel has made possible great shifts of population, while also enabling immigrants to remain in touch with their homelands. The result is that the various branches of the human family are now more exposed to one another than they have ever been before. No longer can any group live isolated in its own homeland, ignorant of and un-influenced by other ways of life. For example, on British television screens we can now watch sophisticated films about Hindu life and thought. In 1983 India's television screens (which are rapidly increasing in number) showed pictures of the Pope forgiving the man who tried to kill him.

Again, next door to the house where I sit typing this essay there lives a family of four Sikh brothers, each married and with his own children, most of whom were born in Britain. Across the road there are three families from the West Indies. Less than five minutes' walk away one can meet Greek Cypriots, Yemeni Arabs, Muslims from Pakistan and Bangla Desh, and Hindus from India.

This state of affairs is exhilarating, for it opens up great new prospects of mutual discovery and enrichment, but at the same time it is disturbing to many people, who feel threatened by the presence of others who are so different from themselves. Indeed in almost every country every group feels that its own identity is threatened, yet at the same time it is itself a threat to the identity of others. Moreover, all societies are being undermined by the secular reductionism which seems invariably to come in the train of material progress.

To illustrate again: near my home is a Sikh temple, housed in a converted church building, a striking symbol to white Christians of the new society in which they now live. Yet as I talk to Sikhs I find that they are themselves deeply troubled about events in their own homeland, the Punjab. Their language, culture and religion are, they feel, menaced by an increasingly vigorous and vociferous Hindu chauvinism. Yet when I lived in Banaras, the most sacred city of the Hindus, a Hindu wrote to the local daily paper urging that no more land be sold to Christians or to Muslims, for the city was in danger of losing its Hindu identity.

Anglicanism is by no means immune to these trends, indeed the resurgence of a conservative theology and the growth of parties in the Church is in a large measure a response to them. At the same time, Christianity is no longer the only or even the obvious religious option for people who live in Britain today. There are now white Hindus, Buddhists, Muslims and Sikhs. Many of the cults which have sprung up in recent years on the edges of the main-line religions can boast of an international clientele.

What effect is this having on the Church of England?

Historically, we have always in some sense been the Church of the nation, closely intertwined with the main elements of its life, and contributors to a Christian ethos which was widely recognized as being at least theoretically normative. The ideal was 'one nation under God'. This was not ignoble, however far reality fell short of the theory.

My years away from this country have perhaps enabled me to perceive the changes more sharply than those who have actually lived through them. The Church of England to which I returned in 1978 was very different from the one I had left in 1965.

Our role in the nation's life is much less dominant than it used to be. One effect of this has been to make us turn in on ourselves and behave more like a sect than a Church whose historic vocation has been to permeate every area of the nation's life. This shows itself in many ways. The Parish Communion is now the central act of worship in most churches, but while this appeals to those who are self-consciously committed, it has led to the disapppearance of matins where those on the fringes were able to feel at home.

Population shifts mean that city churches now have eclectic congregations whose members come either because the particular style of worship and churchmanship appeals to them, or because the church is the one remaining link they maintain with the place in which they used to live. The maintenance of its fabric and of the congregation's life demand a heavy investment of time and money from a dwindling number of people.

The result is that instead of reaching out into the whole life of the area, congregations often look like religious clubs which are interested in very little beyond their own survival. Survival itself is much more complicated than it used to be. Instead of a clergyman to every parish there are now several varieties of team ministry and several different ways of joining parishes together. There is a positive tangle of ministries – stipendiary and non-stipendiary, lay-readers, deacons, deaconesses, priests, all apparently tripping over one another's robes in the sanctuary, all trying to work out how they relate to one another. This can be a much more cosy activity than reaching out in mission to the unchurched or to those of other faiths.

These changes within the Church are symptomatic of wider and deeper changes in society at large. Christian faith and the Christian ethic used to provide Britain with a common language and a common set of values. This did much to shape the ethos of the professions and of politics, but we are now a much more fragmented society. The professions are much more aggressively concerned with their own interests, and politics is much more polarized. The old cultured establishment is vanishing. Even *The Times* has gone 'popular'. We no longer have a common language and this makes it difficult for the Church to speak to the nation with any possibility of being understood, let alone heeded.

The churches which grow are those which offer a clear-cut doctrinal package, a strict moral code, and an authoritarian style of leadership, all of which make for a sharp distinction between Church and world. Many people need this pattern today, at least for a time in the early stages of their pilgrimage, but it is not a pattern which is in any sense Anglican.

Can the Church of England in our inner cities do more than preserve in a comfortable ghetto the remains of a vanished middle class?

I believe that it can if our members, or some of them, can catch a vision of the world-wide fellowship of Christians to which we belong. As I have already suggested, that is no imperialist vision, for the Anglican communion occupies a very modest place in a much larger community. The world-wide fellowship can only be real at a local level if congregations are genuinely multi-racial. In some areas this is already happening, but there is a very long way to go. It is one thing to welcome Asian Christians or black Christians from the West Indies into our congregations on our own terms. It is quite another to enable them to find the freedom and confidence to make their own contribution and perhaps change our way of doing things in the process. Indeed if that is to be even a possibility our unconscious assumptions of superiority and self-sufficiency have to be confessed and done away with. There is much more to this process than might at first sight appear.

Anglicanism in this country has been the dominant form of Christianity since the Reformation. Other Christians are much more aware than we are of just how dominating we are. We need to get beyond the courtesies of ecumenical dialogue and hear what others actually think of us. Overseas too, though we are a minority, we have historic links with Empire – as the crumbling cathedrals and churches of the North Indian plain, and other places, still bear witness.

This intimate link with the dominant and dominating strand of our nation's past imposes on us both a burden and a responsibility. There needs to be a collective healing of our national memory. This alone can save us from the twin evils of a cynical rejection of our past on the one hand, and a jingoistic nostalgia on the other. These two dangers are closely related to the developments in the world scene to which I have already alluded. Rejection of the past goes easily with a secular materialism which is only interested in immediate and superficial gratification. Jingoistic nostalgia means glorying in an imperial past which never really existed. It is an essential element in the cultural and religious fundamentalism which is such a widespread and menacing phenomenon today.

Anglicanism needs to recover and live from the best elements in its own past; it must discover and nourish the sources from which its own memories can find renewal. Only a renewed memory can be an adequate basis for hope. Every community and every individual lives from a story which gives life, direction, continuity and purpose. If our story comes to an end we have nothing before us but chaos and loss of meaning.

Who can deny that this is the state of our nation today? It was also the state of the two disciples on the Emmaus road. According to the story, the risen Christ showed them that it was precisely those elements in their story which they rejected – suffering and loss – which were the seed bed of renewal and hope.

Those who are dominant, as we till recently have been, are always insensitive towards minorities. Change and repentance here could be the beginning of better things. I have already referred to black and to Asian Christians, but more than this, the English have been and still are woefully and culpably ignorant of the history and sensibilities of the Scots, Irish and Welsh. It is, for example, a salutary and humbling lesson to hear what some Welshmen feel about the erosion of their language and distinctive culture before the all-conquering might of English.

We are also ignorant of elements in our own history. My Asian Christian friends living in England will often ask me, with pain and bewilderment on their faces: 'Why does nobody want to know us? Why do all white people think we are Hindus or Muslims? Yet we are the fruit of the labours and sacrifices of the missionaries.' That complaint is profoundly revealing. Neither secular nor ecclesiastical historians have paid serious attention to the great missionary movement which began with the evangelical revival at the end of the eighteenth century. As a result, the very word 'missionary' has no recognized place in our common language. This is just one symptom of the fact that as a nation we have not yet come to terms at a more than superficial level with our own past.

That past haunts us in other ways. When I meet a Sikh for the first time he will often pull out of his pocket the little plastic bag in which he keeps his war medals. These he will proudly display. This is his way of saying: 'I am part of your national story and I have made a positive contribution to it.' Can we find new ways of telling our national story, ways that enable us to include within it the more recent arrivals to our country? On the answer to that question depends the effectiveness or otherwise of the Church of England in inner city areas – and elsewhere.

My Sikh friends are a symbol of other questions which press upon us. The past dominance of Anglicans was part of the widely assumed and largely unquestioned superiority of Christianity to other religions. That superiority is now being challenged and indeed openly rejected, for today we are compelled to meet people of other faiths on a level of equality. In fact, in many inner city areas the roles are now reversed. My Muslim and Sikh friends have watched with amazed incredulity the decline of Christianity over the last twenty years. 'Do you not teach your children anything?' asked a Muslim. 'How can we let our own children loose in a society as corrupt and immoral as yours?'

One of the few readers of *The Times* in this area is a Hindu who came here from East Africa eighteen years ago. He says of the British: 'They have given up their religion and lost their identity. There is too much liberalism.'

More than this, all religions, with the significant exception of Islam, are starting to lose their cohesiveness. I have already pointed to the bewildering variety of cults and fringe movements which are springing up. Their vigorous and exotic life suggests that secular materialism cannot in the end satisfy the human spirit. People are looking for a transcendent dimension to their lives, and are often finding it outside the historic religions. Recently I was asked by a puzzled Asian shop-keeper: 'Do you belong to some religious sect?' That sort of question puts the Church of England firmly in its place.

But what can it contribute to this confused and confusing scene beyond the healing of memories and sensitivity to minorities? For all that survival is not enough, it is for obvious reasons essential. Repetition of the Christian story in office and liturgy can sometimes seem an uninspired and uninspiring routine, yet it may have a power which is greater than we know. In the Gospel story the wise men come to Jerusalem asking where the king of the Jews is to be born. They bring their question to the official guardians of tradition who reply: 'In Bethlehem of Judea.' The guardians do not know how to interpret the information they possess. All they can do is to pass it on. Yet this is the one thing that seekers need to know. That story is a parable. In Moscow, I am told, there is a church to which young people now often come. They are drawn to an icon of the Nativity: 'Who is that woman, and who is the baby?' they ask. To maintain the icons, the liturgy and the holy books may not be particularly exciting, yet that alone can make those kinds of question possible.

Yet Christians have to live outside their buildings as well as within them, and that applies even more to the set of their minds than to the location of their bodies. The Gospel exhorts us to greet all men, not only those like ourselves, for only so can we truly be the children of a heavenly Father whose love is as universal and undiscriminating as the sun and the rain. There needs to be much more meeting with and deep discovery of those who live by different religions. I need the other person to discover who I am. I need to enter into beliefs that are different from mine to discover what my own are. In this kind of encounter the Christian can begin to discover afresh who Christ is and what it means to follow him. He can also find unexpected opportunities of bearing witness to his faith in ways which honour the integrity of others.

But this brings me back to what I wrote at the beginning. We can only explore the unfamiliar if we know where we have come from and to where we hope to return. That implies a deeper grasp of the Anglican inheritance. I believe that inheritance can give us a security which is no retreat into a ghetto, but a liberating experience which can set us free to meet others with confidence and hope.

John Whale

John Whale

⬩⬩⬩

THE MAN WHO MADE me a lifelong Anglican never held any conversation with me, as far as I can remember; and I had no notion of the effect he was producing. I knew him merely as Mr Stallard, a gowned and surpliced figure seen from forty feet away. His full name, I learn from a wartime Crockford's, was Leonard Bristow Stallard: he had been educated, in the last decade of the nineteenth century, at Keble and Cuddesdon (though I can recall no signs of the high-churchmanship which that training might have been expected to bring on); and at the end of forty years divided between country parsonages in Norfolk and Devon he was in his last post. For most of the Second World War he was vicar of the small South Devon town of Ashburton.

As for me, I was a bookish child from Cambridge, where my father and his father-in-law were Congregationalist divines of note. For greater safety from German bombs, the headmaster of my Cambridge prep school carried part of the school into exile at the Golden Lion Hotel (closed to visitors for the duration of the war) in Ashburton; and with a good deal of reluctance my parents sent me to join him.

For three years, between the ages of nine and twelve, I formed part of a crocodile of thirty-odd boys that marched down the hill every Sunday morning in term-time to the parish church. We sat towards the back of its elegant fifteenth-century interior, near one of the octagonal granite pillars that separated the nave from the side-aisles. And we heard Mr Stallard say matins.

'Dearly beloved brethren, the Scripture moveth us in sundry places to acknowledge and confess our manifold sins and wickedness . . .' As I read the service now, more than forty years on, I still hear Mr Stallard's silver voice: educated, unaffected, accurate, catching the emphases of Cranmer's balanced and musical sentences just as Cranmer himself must have heard them in his head: '. . . to render thanks for the great benefits that we have received at his hands, to set forth his most worthy praise, to hear his most holy Word, and to ask those things which are requisite and necessary, as well for the body as the soul.' Free Church worship had already inclined me, I suppose, to be devout at appropriate times. This language, so persuasively spoken, now became for me the one irresistible bidding to devout thoughts. 'Wherefore I pray and beseech you, as many as are here present' (and Mr Stallard could say those words without irony, since we were a decent throng), 'to accompany me with a pure heart and humble voice unto the throne of the heavenly grace, saying after me . . .'

I was a literary child, true. I was already an addict of words. The only books to be found in the Golden Lion were selections from Punch, by subject: *Mr Punch Goes Motoring*, and so on. But the English master brought me Stevenson and Scott and translations of Dumas, with a slight air of contraband, from the Ashburton public library; and I wrote any number of derivative stories in exercise books in pencil. To this temperament, Cranmer's prose – a touch rhetorical, hinting at the magic of the past, setting clear words off with the occasional opacity, negligent of later-invented rules about not mixing up 'which' and 'that' or not ending sentences with prepositions – made immediate and lasting appeal.

Anglicanism remains the literary man's denomination. Of course countless good writers have been members, and a few have been ministers, of either the Free Church or the Roman Catholic tradition in England. But when they have prayed in public, they have used either words composed for the occasion and of uneven merit; or Latin; or – if they are late-twentieth-century Roman Catholics – a leaden English translation from the Latin. Anglicans have had Cranmer: the forms of service which he composed or compiled for the 1549 and the 1552 Book of Common Prayer, and which were transferred with little alteration (and with his influence still strong in any new material) to the 1662. So far from being embarrassed by infelicity, or left unengaged by a foreign tongue, Anglicans have been offered – as long as the minister kept to the words set down for him – prose to charm the most fastidious ear.

Cranmer understood techniques which were used after him by some of the greatest of English poets. He deployed, with all the skill of Vaughan or Tennyson, sequences of long vowels varied in shape: 'Lighten our darkness, we beseech thee, O Lord; and by thy great mercy defend us from all perils and dangers of this night . . .' Notice, too, those first three syllables of 'by thy great mercy'. A succession of three slow, stressed syllables was a device Cranmer especially liked: '. . . and *our souls washed* through his most precious blood'. The rhythm is the same as Othello's line about Desdemona: 'And *I loved her* that she did pity them.' To my ear it is the sound of confident self-surrender.

Cranmer's prose also has an antiphonal quality, serving something of the function of rhyme, in that often it sets up with each phrase an expectation which is delightfully met in the next, and yet the parallel is not completed in every detail, so that the hearer's mind must be alert both in remembering and in looking forward. Witness a prayer it would be an offence not to quote in full:

> Almighty God, the fountain of all wisdom, who knowest our necessities before we ask, and our ignorance in asking: We beseech thee to have compassion upon our infirmities; and those things, which for our unworthiness we dare not, and for our blindness we cannot ask, vouchsafe to give us for the worthiness of thy Son Jesus Christ our Lord.

And all those attributes of verse in Cranmer's prose ensure another, that it is readily memorable; so that the beginning of each phrase suggests to its hearers the end of it, and they are led at once into the way of worshipping because they have been there before.

I know that the opportunity of hearing Cranmer is not now available to all Anglicans. Some of them were deprived of it through the spread of those alternative forms of service that have been gathered together into the Alternative Service Book of 1980. It is difficult to know how widespread this deprivation is. I can speak only out of my own experience. The Book of Common Prayer is still in regular use at many churches in central London (at St Bartholomew the Great, for example, in Smithfield, where I now worship). Bound into it are Coverdale's version of the Psalms, dating from 1540, and readings from the Authorized Version of the Bible, dating from 1611: two works which sometimes enter the argument about Anglican innovation, even though they are not exclusively Anglican. They are cherished also in the Free-Church tradition, where I first learnt snatches of them as a child.

It may be that those lovers of the Book of Common Prayer who gave it up for lost have been too quick despairers: my impression, from encounters with one or two clerics who had dropped it and have taken it up again, is that it is regaining at least a part of the ground it had been driven from. For myself, I feel acutely sorry for those Anglicans who value it and cannot find it used within a manageable distance of where they live. The Alternative Service Book – perhaps because it was the work of many hands, perhaps because the period out of which it came was one when any touch of rhetoric was mistrusted – cannot offer the same satisfactions to the believer's ear as the Book of Common Prayer does. but there are things to be said on the new book's side. The case for making the services of the Church of England readily intelligible to late-twentieth-century newcomers was a cogent one; that case accepted, the process that produced the alternative services was honest and comprehensive; and disproportionate vehemence in denouncing them seems to me out of keeping with one of Anglicanism's historic qualities – its disposition 'to keep the mean', as Sanderson's preface to the 1662 Prayer Book says, 'between the two extremes, of too much stiffness in refusing, and of too much easiness in admitting' changes in the liturgy.

Whether or not it retains its edge in liturgy, the Church of England has another massive advantage: its buildings. A God not made with hands can be worshipped in any building or none: that goes without saying. The fact remains that the accidents of history have left the Church of England the steward of a great many buildings which dispose the heart to worship, and of comparatively few which do not.

Sheer antiquity does much. As you sit under the high Norman arches of St Bartholomew the Great – disproportionately high: the part that survived Henry VIII's dissolution of the monasteries is no more than the choir of what had been a cathedral-sized priory church – you are made aware of an invisible cloud of witnesses: all those plain citizens of London who have come and knelt here over a span of eight hundred years, and (at the lowest) have found the consolations of religion enough to encourage them to keep coming. And antiquity has another message. These buildings have been judged fit to survive. Churches are subject to the same threats as other buildings: in particular, in the City of London, from fire (as in the 1660s and the 1940s) and the pressure for offices. Broadly speaking, the church buildings that survive are the ones that men and women have most valued: have laboured most intently to keep in repair, to renew after mishap, to add to. If they have earned this affection, these buildings can reasonably be taken to be among the best of their period. They are therefore already rich in the dignity and beauty that best frame worship. And those qualities are themselves self-perpetuating: they impose a certain restraint, and yet not too crushing a restraint, on decoration, so that the internal arrangements of Anglican churches strike for the most part a mean between the bareness of certain Free-Church interiors and the lushness of certain Roman Catholic.

I should be uncomfortable, though, if Anglicans did not generally regard these buildings as held in trust for the community at large. A church like St Bartholomew's that was standing before the Reformation was then the church of everyone in the parish. To all intents and purposes there were no rival forms of belief or unbelief. Since the blame for subsequent separations cannot belong entirely to Genevans and Romanists, but must in part also attach to what came to be the Church of England, the Church of England has a continuing obligation towards all those English people who are not its members. Indeed, it acknowledges as much.

It is as a rule disposed to baptize, marry and bury all comers without applying tests of church membership.

Although I understand the hesitation that certain incumbents feel about this easy universalism, it seems to me to be creditable and right. There are many layers of English society where Christian allegiance is not to be measured by churchgoing. The claim of every parish church to be the church even of those parishioners who never attend it is a patient recognition of that fact. The recognition is a source of more pain than satisfaction. Much of this casual ministry of baptisms and weddings produces no detectable growth of Christian life. Again, to allow non-churchgoing parishioners a voice in the parish church's architecture is to court trouble. I bear a few of those bruises myself: a few years ago I was churchwarden at Barnes, in south-west London, when rebuilding plans after a bad fire – they proposed partial demolition of the Victorian and Edwardian work the better to set off the medieval – satisfied the mass of the congregation yet (under the urgings of the remainder) roused a near-insuperable spasm of know-nothing rage in the community outside it. Nevertheless, historically and in law the non-churchgoer has equal rights with the churchgoer, and there is a prudent generosity in conceding them.

Beyond liturgy and buildings, there is something yet more important that attaches me to the Church of England: its tolerance. It is easy enough to say, as many church people of eirenic spirit have said, that in church affairs the great thing is to be firm only about essentials, and libertarian about the rest. But that begs the question of what the essentials are: it sidesteps the problem that different believers identify them differently. The Church of England meets that problem by declaring diversity tolerable.

There is a well grounded hypothesis in mechanics called the uncertainty principle. Devised by a German named Heisenberg, it states the impossibility of measuring both the position and the momentum of a particle simultaneously. The Church of England has extended the uncertainty principle to the core of Christian morality and doctrine; and I am glad that it has.

In morality, I take the example of divorce and remarriage. From the Middle Ages on, Christian teaching made much of the absolute unbreakability of the marriage tie. In the second half of the twentieth century, partly because of a change in women's expectations which itself had Christian elements in it, that doctrine came under strain. A great many marriages did break. Divorce figures multiplied. The point at which this touched the churches was the moment in the 1960s when people who had been married before, and divorced, but who therefore on a strict construction had a spouse still living, began to present themselves in large numbers for a second marriage in church; mainly the parish church.

Civil law allowed an incumbent to perform such a ceremony; Church of England rules, renewed not long before, discouraged him. Clearly it was in the interests of good order that a settled practice should be arrived at, so that everybody could know where they stood. For the best part of twenty years the Church of England struggled to reach a common mind. The difficulty was that the old tripod to which Anglicanism looked for support – scripture, tradition and reason – could not sustain a firm answer. Scripture, even supposing we could be sure it told us what Jesus really said, did not make clear whether what he said about the unbreakability of marriage was a counsel of perfection or a statement of metaphysical fact. Tradition was divided: although the Christian Church had preached metaphysical indissolubility since the Middle Ages, it had not done so before. Reason was similarly inconclusive: you either showed mercy to the divorced, or by taking a hard line you helped those in danger of divorce to stand against it, but you could not do both. Certainty that you were right was not to be had.

Various systems were mooted for discriminating between one case and another according to some central code. They could none of them command a solid majority of Church of England opinion, as measured in diocesan synods and the General Synod. At length, early in 1985, the bishops declared that they would no longer resist the incumbent's right to judge each case as he thought fit, whatever the rules said; and the General Synod came in behind. It was an acknowledgment that general certainty on the point was not to be looked for: an acceptance of the uncertainty principle.

In doctrine, I take an example of supreme importance: the nature of the resurrection. 'The third day he rose again from the dead . . .' It is probably true that most Christians have taken those words from the Apostles' Creed literally, and still do. In their mind's eye they have seen a physical process: a body sitting up, standing . . . Although such a sequence is not set out in the New Testament stories of the empty tomb and the post-resurrection appearances, it can be squared with them. On the other hand, in the past 150 years Western scholars in a number of disciplines have been systematically pointing out that we no longer need the hypothesis of the miraculous to understand anything else about our world, past or present; that standards of evidence and historical truth in the ancient world were different from standards now; and that even if we take at face value the New Testament accounts of the post-resurrection appearances – on the Emmaus road, for example, or the

Damascus road (an occasion which Paul represents as having been on all fours with the others) – they were not of a Jesus in precisely the bodily form his disciples had previously known. Noting all that, a good many Christians have preferred to understand those accounts not so much literally as metaphorically.

In this country, the scholars who took the lead in that kind of approach to the New Testament have for the most part been members of the Church of England. Some of them have become bishops. The earliest was Hampden at Hereford in 1848; the most recent has been Jenkins at Durham in 1984. Sometimes, at the point of consecration, there has been a fuss: it has invariably been contained, and as a rule the bishop under question, being a man of character and courage – a Gore, a Henson – has gone on to become a loved national figure.

I am myself happy to be a member of a Church that arranges its affairs with this degree of wisdom. The plain fact, which one need not be a scholar to perceive, is that the evidence about the resurrection can be read either way. Some Christians follow a literal interpretation; some prefer a metaphorical; some find in themselves a continuing sympathy for both readings. And these questions are not to be settled by authority; still less by synodical vote. The believing heart does not take dictation. All this the Church of England perceives. By accommodating diversity of belief it accepts that uncertainty is unavoidable.

Morality, doctrine: if we were using the term 'Anglican' strictly, of the world-wide body, we could make the same case about church order. Take the priesthood of women. It raises questions about the nature of Christian priesthood which Christianity's foundation documents cannot certainly settle. World-wide Anglicanism acknowledges the uncertainty by settling the question differently in different provinces: women are ordained to the Anglican ministry in Canada, for example, yet not in England. But for the purposes of this chapter I have been using 'Anglican' (in common, I dare say, with most other writers in this book) as if it were the adjective from 'Church of England'; and the Church of England, facing its own problems about the ministry of women, is not yet ready to adopt even a patchy solution.

'It is the nature of all greatness,' said Burke, 'not to be exact.' He was advocating a system of taxation whereby the American colonies should be allowed, within the limits set by their own past fidelity, to pay what they liked. The idea was unpopular. The Church of England has had similar difficulties about letting people believe what they liked, within the same limits. From the first it has had members who found its careful comprehensiveness unsatisfactory. Queen Elizabeth I intended, in her settlement of 1559, an arrangement whereby the reformed Church of England should remain the sole Church of the nation, to which everyone could more or less comfortably belong. But determined Roman Catholics were uneasy from the first, and (partly as a result of papal policy) withdrew within a dozen years into active separatism; and determined Genevans – Free Church people – began a hundred years after that the process of setting up their own ministry and their own churches. Among those who stayed with the Church of England there were always activists who wanted to pull the main body across the middle line into exclusive sympathy with Rome or Geneva. It has gone on happening. The struggles of the seventeenth century were renewed, though with less bloodshed, in the nineteenth, especially over ritual; and they persist, in just such matters as marriage discipline or the priesting of women, into the late twentieth.

Believers must do what their consciences bid them. But my own disposition is to be saddened by these continuing attempts to narrow the Church of England's compass. I believe that it has been the Church of England's peculiar genius, ever since the Elizabethan settlement, to be all-embracing; and that to misunderstand that is greatly to limit the Church of England's opportunities for service. I believe this to be especially true in matters of doctrine, the ground of all other disputes. The Church of England was a monument, long before Mill, to Mill's simple principle: 'We can never be sure that the opinion we are endeavouring to stifle is a false opinion.' The Elizabethans had more temptation to feel sure about religion than we have. They did not have our disadvantages. They could still maintain that tradition or Scripture was infallible. We know that we cannot know that: we have begun to learn how much of both was man-made to meet the needs of a specific time and place. All the more ought we to be tolerant of diverse interpretations.

One practical argument is brought against that kind of comprehensiveness: the ecumenical one. If the Church of England goes on straddling the divide between Rome and Geneva, it cannot expect unity with the one or the other. Either the Protestant or the Catholic tendency within the Church of England cannot be carried along, and the proposed new partner will perceive that. The argument is sound enough, and seems to me unimportant. Ecumenism itself is a forlorn prospect, and hardly deserves to be more. The whole history of the Christian faith indicates that there are thousands of ways of believing. The best that can be established between them is mutual respect and charity: a recognition that one group's way of treating sacrament or belief or ministry may be as valid as another's. The Church of England already offers, on a comparatively small scale, a pattern of the kind of permissive churchmanship which expresses that charity. It would be odd, as a step towards more of that permissiveness, to dismantle what little of it we already have.

What would I be if I were not an Anglican? Beyond question, I should still be a Free Churchman, and of the United Reformed stripe (the label that now covers Congregationalism): adhering, like most Christians, to the denomination I happened to be born in. Indeed, I retain a certain shame at not being in it now. Another cloud of witnesses compasses me about – smaller than I encounter at St Bartholomew's, but with a closer claim on me: my father's father, dead long before my birth, who left a wheelwright's shop on Bodmin Moor to work his way through preacher's college in Ontario, returning to a chapel ministry in Cornwall and Devon; my mother's father, whose house and daily walks in Cambridge I constantly saw crowded with the friends he served; my father, *verbi divini minister* if ever I heard or read one; my mother, who out of all the Bible taught me to recite that proof text of the divine mercy, the 103rd Psalm ('Look how wide also the east is from the west: so far hath he set our sins from us . . .'). How could I say that their ministry was in the smallest degree misplaced? Switching churches is not delivered from that touch of ugliness which any change of allegiance carries. In the days when people transferred from chapel to church as a means or sign of going up in the world, the move was merely contemptible. If it were now undertaken in the belief that one denomination commanded more of the truth than another, it would be a piece of intellectual presumption. We cannot know. When I was confirmed in the school chapel by the saintly Bishop Mervyn Haigh of Winchester, I was at any rate still young enough to be innocent of those offences. I was doing no more than following out the accidents of where and what I was. Yet I was leaving behind a great inheritance.

The dissenting tradition in England has been immeasurably precious. It won us freedom of worship: not the fiercest devotee of the 1662 Book of Common Prayer would now wish to see penalties exacted for worshipping without the book, yet that is what nonconformists chose to suffer for a century and a half till the penalties were lifted. It gave the humble and meek a place to worship where their equality with the mighty in the sight of God was real; whereas when the Church of England drew the poor to church at all, it confined them for long years in the back pews. Dissent was an indispensable engine in the movement of ordinary people towards their political rights: it filled the parliamentary ranks in the Civil War, it was a leading force behind the passing of the Reform Bill and the setting up of trade unions, it provided nearly all the first Labour MPs.

Nevertheless, if you have once left that fold, those achievements are not a reason to go back into it now. That work is done. Freedom of religion in England is a fact: not merely have nonconformists liberated themselves from Anglican forms of worship, but they have altered those forms in their own direction by teaching Anglicans to sing hymns. Again, consciousness of class in the Church of England has fallen to as low a level as human nature permits: certainly to a lower level than in the nation at large. When my father's father was the Congregationalist minister in Buckfastleigh (the next town to Ashburton, it so happens, down the Plymouth road), the vicar would scarcely give him good morning. Nowadays there is unaffected friendliness almost everywhere between Church of England and nonconformist clergy, and Church of England congregations unite as wide a range of classes as any voluntary body in the land.

There is another side to that picture, though. The Congregationalist church in Buckfastleigh has been closed for ten years. The decline in numbers of adherents that has afflicted virtually all English denominations in the past fifty years has borne particularly hardly on nonconformity. To all the other reasons for decline has been added precisely this perception that the work of dissent is done.

Even so, one of the principles of Free Churchmanship is still unmet by Anglicanism: that a Church should not be subject to any control or interference by the state. The Church of England cannot yet pass that test. Notably, the state retains a certain influence over the character of the Church of England's leaders. When bishops are to be appointed, a church commission is the sole source of names; but the prime minister has a power of veto before a name goes forward to the monarch for approval. For the most part, beyond doubt, the veto is not in question and the Church of England is straightforwardly choosing its own leaders. But human nature would be other than it is if there were not sometimes instances when members of the commission drew back from proposing a certain name because it would be troubling to the prime minister in power. In very rare instances, that might be the name the Church of England needed.

Commissioners would draw back because they knew that if they pressed the issue they might be raising the whole question of establishment. The Church of England's residual position as the national Church is not something which on the whole its supporters are yet ready to see given up. Periodic agitation for disestablishment comes to nothing. A good many people, inside and outside the Church of England, still like its being the national Church for the decent reason that they like belonging to a nation which has a national Church. Among the Church's senior ·professionals, a further persuasion is the fact of having bishops and archbishops in the Lords. It is the one identifiable privilege of establishment, and it does allow a specifically Christian voice to be heard in Parliament.

I am not myself persuaded. I remain enough of a Free Churchman to think that a body of believers should be answerable to God and no one else; that the Church of England continues to colour the national life not through any standing as the national Church but through the lives of its faithful ministers and people; and that having a number of its bishops in Parliament does not advance its work so well as choosing them uninhibitedly would. Yet just as time has removed the spectacle of prime ministers choosing bishops for party purposes, and has since then reduced prime ministerial choice to a mere veto, so time can be trusted to dismantle the rest of the apparatus of establishment. And I would not contend that lawn sleeves in the Lords are an important hindrance to the Church of England's continuing usefulness.

Tommy Dingsdale
MBE

Tommy Dingsdale MBE

I WAS BORN IN THATTO HEATH, a district of St Helens –
then in Lancashire, now in Merseyside. I was soon to
come to terms with the real world. My father and both
grandfathers were coalminers; grandfather Dingsdale had
sustained a broken back while working in the mines.
Consequently, he spent the rest of his life in a wheelchair.
People were very poor moneywise, but rich in everything
else. Each day, except Sunday, the community put aside
their own religions and attended the Salvation Army Cita-
del for a sing-song; then a bowl of soup and a piece
of bread. Honesty prevailed everywhere, with everyone
willing to help with any problems large or small. Growing
up in this kind of society made a deep impression on me,
and although I didn't see it then, I know now, they were
all basically Christians. I was baptized an Anglican at
Ravenhead, St John's, where, incidentally, I was married.
During the 1926 General Strike, at the age of seven years,
I had to walk about one and a half miles to where my
father was digging for open cast coal. I wheeled an old
perambulator for my father to transport home a couple of
bags of coal so as to keep our home fire burning. The fire
not only kept the family warm, but enabled my mother to
cook whatever food was available. Any bags of coal, other
than the two for home, would be sold for one shilling to
one of the three businessmen found at the site. These people

had transport, in the form of a horse and cart, to convey the coal to the few people who had the means to pay one pound per bag.

Because I played soccer and cricket for Balmer Street Methodist Church, I attended firstly the Sunday school and then, secondly, the Bible class there.

At school – Thatto Heath Council – I was only average academically, but was good at sports, being captain of cricket and rugby, and also vice-captain of soccer. My only real contribution was the fact that during a rugby match I kicked eight goals out of eight with clogs on. My family at the time, as with lots of other families, were too poor to buy football boots; we played in the clogs we had for everyday wear.

Shortly after the season started, the authorities banned clogs from the playing field, saying they were too dangerous. My record of goals with clogs on can never be equalled, so perhaps it will go down in history. Friends and relatives later collected enough to buy me football boots, but then I was unfortunate enough to break my leg. Every night I had several visitors of my own age who came to cheer me up; it always ended up with one of them borrowing my boots.

When I was young I had little time for religion because I was feeling bitter about the treatment which my family in particular, and the community in general, were being subjected to. Then, as now, people said, 'What kind of God could allow such a division in society of very rich and very poor?'

My wife is also an Anglican and we married during the war while I was serving as a navigator in Bomber Command. I prayed several times while flying, but only because, at the time, I feared death.

Tall, dark and handsome would have gained me no

marks out of three, so perhaps God thought I deserved something when he changed my life in 1977.

I had joined the Amalgamated Engineering Union at the age of fourteen when I started my apprenticeship but was never interested in holding any office, until at the age of thirty I was talked into being a shop steward. Later I became Works Convenor, which is one of the quickest ways to learn how queer folk can be. After a somewhat hesitant start, I began to trust the managing director, and, better still, he trusted me. In the twenty years I held this office we never had a works strike and I firmly believe that *trust* is the one thing which is missed most in the world and not just by unions and employers.

After a motor-cycle accident my arm was permanently injured, and I found it difficult to carry on in heavy engineering. I had always been interested in helping apprentices and so, at the age of forty-nine, I moved to a job in an apprentice training school. My workmates, and, even more, the management, didn't want me to leave. They offered all kinds of alternative work in the hope that I would continue, but I had a very strong feeling that I had to move. God works in mysterious ways, I have heard said many times, and my story will certainly prove it.

The training school and life continued as normal until Friday, 13 May, one week before my fifty-eighth birthday. The manager sent for me and said that because of its cost the directors of the firm had decided to close the apprentice school at the completion of the present year. I would be redundant as from August. Anyone made redundant will know the feeling I had at that moment. At fifty-eight, where would I get another job? I remember leaving the manager's office to his words: 'Every possible earthly thing has been done.' As I stumbled out on to the football field which it had taken me three years to gain for the school, I took my first steps to becoming an Anglican again.

I prayed in the middle of the field and felt, as I have felt many times since, that I was alone talking to God and he was listening: 'Oh God, they say every possible earthly thing has been done, will you please answer me the heavenly way? I have not done a lot for you, but will you help me to keep the school going and therefore help trainees to acquire some skills with a view to finding jobs which are disappearing fast? Also help the staff in their time of trouble and show you are with us in all walks of life.' Not much of a prayer you may think, but what an answer I received.

Feeling better after the prayer, I returned to the school with the name David Sheppard going round in my head. This was the name of our bishop, but I only knew him as an ex-England cricketer. Suddenly it came to me that the David Sheppard I was thinking of was the managing director of one of the large firms in St Helens. He was also the chairman of a committee of which I was a member, and we met every two months. I decided to phone him. His secretary told me that he was attending a special meeting with the other directors, because of the possibility that their firm would have to close. She got my message to him and to my surprise he answered immediately, enquiring what I wanted – and telling me to make it quick. I told him that our school was closing and that I wasn't sure why I was phoning him; he, to say the least, got really mad. 'We may be closing and you interrupt me during the meeting, and now you don't know exactly what for!' he said.

I explained about the prayer and his name, to which he replied: 'Am I the answer to your prayer?'

'Not if you ring off,' I remember blurting out to him.

We talked for almost twenty-five minutes, and, considering how busy he was, I felt that God was already at work. He contacted the Job Centre manager, a Bruce Caulfield, who came to the school to help us in our fight. He contacted a Jim Forsythe, secretary to St Helens Trades Council, who phoned to say that he would see me on the following Monday, as he was just on his way to a meeting in London. On Monday morning I answered the phone to a Dewi Rees, calling from London. He had sat next to Jim Forsythe at that London meeting. He was impressed by the school and my prayer, and wished to meet me in Liverpool. Two days later we met and I became aware that he was a top officer in the Manpower Services Commission. He was willing to continue running the school, but stipulated that we must do projects for the community – for example, for churches, youth clubs and community centres – while practising the engineering skills. Because of the revival of the school, I received a lot of publicity in the local newspapers. I also spoke on Radio Mersey, referring all the time to answered prayer. Offers to be on this and that committee ended up with my being on twenty-six, some church and others union and politics. I was delighted to accept an offer from Bishop David Sheppard to serve on the Urban Priorities Committee and meet people with whom I could discuss the Church and the *real world*. My union training and the knowledge that God was with me helped to make it a success. As an executive member of the St Helens Trades Council, I found myself in a predicament when asked to attend a 'sit-in' at a factory where the police were to issue an eviction order. My feelings were with the workers, mostly women, who had been subjected to a very raw deal: but being also a committed Christian I had to think of all the parties concerned: workers, management and police. The Rev. Ted Longman, my vicar, a few others and I prayed in St Philip's, my church, on the morning of the eviction day. We prayed for all concerned, and later I was told that the police left the site after a chat with those who were at the sit-in. Next day everything was resolved as another company, impressed by the workers' determination, did a take-over.

The next test of my faith was the nurses' strike or what was called a Day of Action. Being a member of the union, I was now a chairman of my branch AUEW and TASS and also executive of the Trades Council. I was supposed to go on a 'demo' but because of my commitment to the trainees in the school, who were not supposed to go on strike, this caused a problem. I decided to organize a church service at St Philip's to which I invited leaders of other denominations, and of course the trainees. Everyone lost one hour's pay. Most of the trainees attended, thinking perhaps that it was a break from school. A month later two of the trainees said they wanted to go back to their schools to sit A-Levels and enter the Church full-time. The service had made an impression on them.

Since we had not had a holiday for a few years, my wife, daughter and myself booked for Bulgaria. Friends warned me not to keep talking to the people of that country about my church activities, but to inform them only of my union office. My family's advice was to have a rest and to forget all the work that I was doing – and this was what I decided to do. Watching a film about Bulgaria, past and present, whilst I was in the country, I was puzzled when they referred to towns being built in such a year BC and some in such a year AD. If they didn't recognize Christ, I asked, how could they use him as a point of reference? My question appeared to surprise them, but surprises were also in store for me.

Children in Bulgaria commence school at the age of seven years, but religion is never taught, so I was informed.

The state pays nothing to the churches, and religion is never encouraged. 'Are you a paid member of the Church of England?' they asked.

'No,' I replied.

'Well what is your paid occupation?' they said.

They were very interested when I replied that I taught engineering skills to young people. When I was asked about my interests or hobbies, I then told them of all the committees: Church, Unions, Trade Councils, Education, etc.

Looking puzzled they asked how I could represent both the churches and the unions.

I answered them that in church, the congregation prays for the unemployed and I ask the Lord to give me guidance to help them through the union. I said that this was one instance where I linked the spiritual with the practical, and there were also others.

After further conversation on the Church and the union, I was asked whether I had been on the radio in England, and when I said I had, they asked me to speak on Varna Radio. The cathedral and churches in Varna were shown to me and I was impressed by the people who build, maintain and pray in them. Compared to what it must cost them financially, on top of the hassle from the state, my contribution to the Church seemed somewhat meagre. Having gone to Bulgaria just for a rest, and then having become so involved, it brought home the saying that God works in mysterious ways.

Another instance of the union and my religion combining came at a Trades Council Executive Meeting in the St Helens Town Hall. Before the meeting, at night, one of our local papers, *The Star*, featured me on the front page regarding the prayers and the real world. My photograph was accompanied by the headline PRAYER POWER TOM together with an account of some of my activities.

One of the committee was a communist, and the others were for the hard left, and not really the types to give religion much thought. Knowing what I would have to face if I attended the meeting, I thought at first that it would be better to stay away until the story subsided somewhat – the next meeting in a month's time would be ideal. Feeling something of a coward if I didn't attend, I prayed about it, asking God to be there. I felt it was me and God against them. When I arrived very little was said as we awaited the arrival of the chairman. The chairman failed to appear so one of the other members had to be voted on by the rest of the executive. Knowing that I was the odd one out, and feeling that they would vote for one of themselves, I sat back and waited for them to decide who was to take the chair. Much to my surprise, the communist member proposed me, and it was seconded by the most extreme left-winger one could meet. Rising to the chair I closed my eyes and thanked God for being with me. Sitting down somewhat dazed, I heard the seconder say that he had seen my photo in the paper and read of my other activities. He had spoken to people about the article, saying he was a friend of mine and proud to be associated with me. After the meeting I approached the communist, saying that I was surprised he proposed me as we appeared to have different views on life. He explained that from the age of five, he had spent seven heartbreaking years in a religious orphanage. At the age of twelve he had run away and lived very rough in Liverpool dockland, fed by the dockers. He started work at fifteen but never really forgave religion for those first years in the world. After reading about my kind of religion and what God was doing in the real world, he was starting to view life a little differently. We chatted for over an hour on the town hall steps and he quoted many passages from the Bible. Gradually he faded out of the press, which had given him a hard time, and he also dropped off some of the committees. A short while after this occurred, I was informed that he had become a Christian again. I prayed that night and thanked God for all he was doing for the people who spoke first – and then listened to him.

Another example of God's guiding hand at work happened with one of the work force, this time a joiner. He would work overtime, without pay, to finish a job. If the job was too large for the joiners' shop, he would work outside in the rain or snow or whatever. He would put up with anything because he was frightened of losing his job, so it was a terrible blow when he was made redundant. He came to me in deep distress that after all he had done for the firm he was now no longer required. Aged in his late forties, he felt like I did when faced with looking for another job. Having read my story of prayer and then a new life, he came to me for comfort.

'Go and pray about it and put it in the hands of the Lord and I will pray for you as well,' was my message of comfort to him. A month later I thought I saw him leave a car and enter a house but it was only a view of his back, so I waited for him to leave (as I was a bit nosey). It was him, and when he saw me he came dashing over to shake my hand very excitedly, filling me in on his activities of the preceding month. He had been to the Job Centre for two weeks and was then offered the job of checking repairs on houses. The rent man would make a note of the repairs quoted by the tenant, and my former work-mate had the job of checking their authenticity. He regretted all the years that he had spent worrying about his job. He realized that it was so unnecessary to worry.

'You are like me,' I said. 'We should have come to know and trust the Lord a lot sooner.'

Most of the events covering the last few years started with a prayer and were then followed by action of some kind on my part. But the next revelation was prayer and God did the rest. My vicar, Ted Longman, and a few others from my church, St Philip's, went to view a community centre and church to see if it would be possible for our area to develop something on the same lines. Our church is a wooden building, built in 1939, with a life-span of about ten years, so we are naturally concerned about the future. Since we live in an urban priority area, we thought that if a building was available, money could be obtained from the diocese to convert it into a community centre and that the plans could provide for a future extension to be added: a church to replace our wooden building.

Firstly, a labour club became vacant, close to our church, but because so many different organizations had a share in it, the building was unsuitable and adapting it would be too expensive.

Next, wonder of wonders, a large garage which had housed a few coaches, became vacant, so enquiries started again. As it was a fairly new building, it was sold before we could take any real action. Shortly after, it was up for sale again as the first deal fell through. Again, a person bought it with an offer which we couldn't match, but once again the deal fell through, because of some legal fault. All the while we were praying and asking the Lord to guide us, and the next thing to happen was that the building was offered to the church at a reasonable price. The vicar then put in a lot of work and eventually, the diocese gave the go-ahead. The next set-back was when we were told that the roots from the huge tree at the side of the building would have to be removed if the building was to be safe for the future. Enquiries told us that the tree was a couple of hundred years old and therefore we were not allowed to cut it down, nor destroy its roots. More prayer followed with lots of heart-searching, and we told God that this was the last straw – almost.

A few nights later, with a strong gale blowing, the tree was blown down. The realists told us that the wind must have come from an unusual angle, hit the wall, bounced back and hit the tree with hidden force! The vicar and I truly believe that it was God's work and nothing short of a miracle.

God had done so many things in my life, and I was positive he was there again. People of little faith tried to convince me that all the things that happened were just coincidences, but I am convinced that we have a real and listening God.

Mike Walsh, the ITV producer, came to my home to talk about the school where I was the senior instructor. He came to realize the problems that teenagers have in receiving training and obtaining employment. The trainees in the school later appeared on *TV Eye* to tell their own story so that the rest of society would perhaps recognize their plight.

1984 would be my year to retire. I reached the age of sixty-five in the May of that year. With the school behind me, what, I thought, would God have planned for me, if anything? Towards the end of 1983 I was thanking God for all that had happened in the last few years. I hoped he understood that I couldn't just sit back and rest. In late November, I received a letter asking if I would accept an MBE were it to be offered me in the New Year Honours list.

'What have I done to deserve such an award?' was my first thought when I got over the shock. My family, who were the only ones in the know, persuaded me to accept, reminding me of all the nights I was away from home, on

all the committees, without pay. It was given because of
all the community work I was doing, plus the fact that 600
trainees had started regular employment. What a climax to
seven years of what should really have been the lost years.

My last revelation is what I firmly believe to be the key
to my success in being an Anglican and the spin-off to life
in general. One word – *trust* – is the answer. First, your
trust in God, and then the world's trust in you. One of the
workers on the site, but not in the school, asked me to
attend a meeting involving himself and his management
because there was a dispute on. I had to remind him that I
neither worked for his firm nor was I a member of his
union. When he revealed that he would feel happier if I
was present, because he trusted me, I decided to go. The
management wanted to know what I was doing at the
meeting and my colleague explained that it was at his
suggestion. They remarked that they knew all about my
beliefs and activities and would be happy for me to stay as
they trusted me.

Most of the negotiations between unions and management break down because of a lack of trust, so the Church,
in my view, has a role to play in the real world. Christians
in industry must make their voices heard, informing others
of a listening and ever-present God. The clergy should be
seen to be bringing God to people in all walks of life –
today – and not be always talking about events of almost
two thousand years ago. People repeatedly said to me,
when first reading about my church activities, 'I didn't
know you were religious as you are always laughing and
joking.' Compared with a few years ago, when there
appeared to be so much gloom, today there seem to be
only a few church members who never try to put on a
smile and who look as if they don't enjoy church. Members
of the congregation say that they don't know enough about

religion to go out and spread the Gospel. Go out and let people know that you attend church, look happy about it and win their trust. This is a good way to start God's work.

My revelations are about the present time because I too feel that I don't know enough about the Bible and events long ago. One night, I came home from a meeting at half past eleven at night to be informed by my wife that a drunk had been ringing every thirty minutes enquiring where I was. He rang again shortly after I arrived home, saying he had read about me and asking if I would help him to stop wasting his life. Although it was late, and because he lived nearby, I went round to talk to him. Having talked about the great happenings in my life, we arranged to meet at the church on Sunday. We shared a joke and he liked the atmosphere – and I'm happy to say that he is now a Christian.

During my travels I have found that the Anglican faith provides the Church for all people and places. People have revealed that they were happy in such a church but unhapy in another. Some people prefer the high church, others prefer what I would call the average one, and finally others, like myself, the wooden hut type with chairs instead of pews. I think it wrong when people put emphasis on the style of the building, and the sort of vicar. The knowledge that God is everywhere and love for the rest of the congregation is my idea of Christianity. Looking back on my life, the advice I offer most is: *trust* in God and *talk* to him in prayer. Everyone, I am sure, has worried about something or other and not shared it with God. Would I pass exams at school? Would I get a job? Would I come through the war alive? Would I be a success at the training school? All worries are so unnecessary, and at the age of fifty-eight years, I was given the answer. Hopefully, people reading this will come to the Lord a lot sooner and enjoy his gift of life for a longer period before being called to him and life ever after.

Since retiring (if such a thing exists) I go around talking to various organizations, some connected to the Church, others not, about my previous seven years. It gives me great pleasure to talk to the people in the day schools. The response I receive makes it all worth while. The teenagers continue to receive my help, as I am on more committees.

These are the revelations of a happy Anglican whose only regret was that he did not go to God a lot sooner.

Frank Field MBE

Frank Field MBE

WHY SHOULD a Labour MP be contributing to a series of religious essays, let alone setting out on public display why he is an Anglican? The Labour Party has always acknowledged its debt to Christianity, but more recently Marxism has become a dominant philosophy amongst Labour activists. And, as far as the Church of England goes, for generations we have been told it is nothing but the Tory Party at prayer.

The first part of this question can be answered succinctly. I believe that religious issues are of primary importance and that political matters can never be more than secondary. Indeed, political debate gains its importance only by its religious and moral significance. Take unemployment for example. It is one of the major injustices in my constituency (and in all too many others). I feel passionately about its destructiveness because the dole queues stand in daily defiance of what the Church teaches as God's order for this world.

Why I am an Anglican – rather than a Roman or a Methodist – requires a somewhat longer answer. I have no grand theoretical views, like the *via media*, as to why I hold to this part of the Church. In essence there are two reasons. First, I was born an Anglican, and being an Anglican gives an appealing shape to my religious life. This Anglican appeal touches on the ceremonial, the language, and the sounds which men and women have built up over time as they have attempted to express the great truth. All this forms a tradition which is alive and developing; so while I am critical of the destructiveness of recent liturgical reforms, I don't believe these criticisms should be over-emphasized. To do so is insulting to the intelligence and good sense of one's fellow pew-dweller. Nevertheless, to take just one example, no amount of socializing (if such a word is allowed in a volume which has A. N. Wilson contributing) will make the plain dottiness and banality of much of *A hundred hymns for today* appear anything than what they are. I realize, however, that the patterns of beauty in Anglicanism hold primarily a personal appeal and I am enough of a Tractarian to know the value of reserve and not to over-emphasize this dimension of my faith.

Secondly, I am still an Anglican because of what I believe the Church has the potential to become and to achieve. I remain in the Church of England because I believe it has a particular evangelizing role to fulfil, one which no other Church is in a position to take on: that peculiar role arises out of its status as a national Church.

Later in this essay, I will focus on those resources in the Church which give me hope for a renewal of the Church's national mission. But honesty demands that an answer to the question, 'Why am I still an Anglican?' be preceded by a more troubling one, 'What factors strain my allegiance to the Anglican Church?'

The most important factor for me has been the growing sectarianism which sees the Church's mission as tied up exclusively with the elect, the faithful, the committed, or whatever term you wish to use for a limited but dedicated congregation. Sectarianism has had a profound effect on the liturgical life of the Church. The parish communion movement, for instance, has brought an important liturgi-

cal innovation which rightly emphasized the Church's sacramental role; but, as the reforms spread from parish to
parish, the effect was to disenfranchise, or at least put a
hurdle before, the three quarters of the baptized membership of the national Church who were not confirmed.

These liturgical reforms culminated in the adoption of
the Alternative Service Book – another signpost along the
route from the status of national Church to that of a
Christian sect. These experiments have resulted in the
disenfranchising of the outer group of adherents – those
who occasionally come to church and who are at a loss to
comprehend the new rite.

If the movement towards exclusive and divisive sectarianism remains unchecked, the reformers within the
Church of England will soon begin to insist also that the
Church's ministry should be redirected away from
the whole parish and become concentrated exclusively on
the elect.

The sectarian tendencies should be resisted not only on
theological grounds; that sectarianism is in direct opposition to the comprehensive appeal of the Gospels – but
also because a diminished national role for the Church of
England will lessen the impact it could or should be having
on helping the country think through the major issues
which face it in the light of the Gospel.

That gives the depressing side of the picture. Now what
are the resources that allow me to give a hopeful answer
to the question, 'Why am I still an Anglican?'

I am still an Anglican because of the Church's intimacy
with the culture of the nation. Over many centuries, Anglicanism has managed to construct a religious scaffolding
linking the basically flawed nature of man with his hope
for eternity. And it has achieved this in a way which makes
a special appeal to English men and women. It is not only

that the English Church is woven into the fabric of our country's history, but that this very historical tradition has allowed the Church to develop an interpretation of the world and eternity which accommodates English sensibilities. As such it has an advantageous position for any evangelizing role. Trying to fulfil this role is what makes the Church of England a national Church.

Of course, the Church's claim to be national is closely bound up with its establishment status. Critics would argue that a link with powerful interests cuts the Church off from the dispossessed. But I believe this is to misunderstand the relationship that is involved. There is all the difference in the world between an established church and an establishment church. It is undeniable that the Church of England has acted too often in the past as an establishment church. But I do not believe this is inevitable. Being established can enable and encourage the Church to speak to and for the nation, to be the prompter of its conscience. That it can no longer do so uncontroversially is to my mind an argument in favour of continued establishment. Think, for example, of the Archbishop of Canterbury's sermon at the Falklands Thanksgiving Service. Would the sermon have had the impact it did, would the Archbishop have been able to touch the moral nerve of the nation, if the Church had not been in the relationship of critical solidarity with the state that is implied in Establishment?

I am still an Anglican because I believe that a national Church is best placed to be theologically comprehensive and liturgically inclusive. It will give equal importance to a number of doctrines: the creation, the incarnation, the fall and redemption, but if these are given disproportionate emphasis, the doctrines become ones which strengthen the Church's exclusiveness, rather than emphasizing the universality of its message. To prevent this happening, it is critically important for these two doctrines to be run in harness with the doctrines of creation – that the whole world was made by God – and of the incarnation, which stresses how God's becoming human makes *all* that goes on in the world of concern to God.

Liturgical inclusiveness is on the defensive in the Church at present. But I cannot but hope that this setback is temporary, for this inclusiveness is vital to the continuance of the Church's proper mission. The Prayer Book has for so long been the liturgical model for that inclusiveness. It has provided a flexible enough nexus of beliefs to hold together the different church parties, while at the same time providing that minimum of doctrine necessary to give members the sense of belonging to a distinct part of the universal Church. Whatever the future of the liturgy, we must recover the inclusive mentality that the Prayer Book has symbolized.

I am still an Anglican because I believe the Church of England is best placed to respond to the elements of folk or popular Christianity that prevail in this country. The decline in participation in 'rites of passage' such as baptism, confirmation and church weddings, has been interpreted simply as evidence of secularization. I believe a very different interpretation of these figures can be offered. For centuries, it is alleged, the Church of England has been seen in the eyes of the common people as being closely allied with the most powerful and law-enforcing groups in our society. Local clergymen have taken their place on the bench and, if they have not dispensed justice more toughly than their lay colleagues, they were rarely noted for being more charitable. For centuries too the English clergy had a responsibility for raising much of their own income from glebe lands and were also responsible for levying the church rate and, if need be, enforcing payment. Since the last century the Church has had great difficulty winning adherence among town dwellers. Yet, despite this record, over a third of all babies – including those whose parents adhere to other parts of the Church – are still being presented for baptism in the Church of England. Likewise with confirmation: despite all our failings, sizeable numbers of young children still come forward to be confirmed in the Church of England. And the marriage figures are even more remarkable. Once those marriages that cannot take place in church are excluded we see that the numbers of first marriages taking place in the Church of England remain around the 50% mark – as it did in the 1950s – which is itself a rate not far below the World War I level.

All too often participation of this kind is categorized as mere folk religion, as if such a categorization somehow automatically disqualified it from serious consideration. There are, thankfully, exceptions to this approach. In a recently published book, the Archbishop of York looks sympathetically at 'the unexpressed, inarticulate, but often deeply felt, religion of ordinary folk who would not usually describe themselves as church-going Christians yet feel themselves to have some sort of Christian allegiance' (*Church and Nation in a Secular Age*, Darton, Longman & Todd, p. 78). I believe that a Church confident of its obligations to the nation can capitalize on such evidence of popular Christianity.

I am still an Anglican because its material and human resources give it hope of fulfilling its national mission. Church buildings are crucial in providing the physical base from which the Church's mission is carried out. While the number of church buildings is on the decline, very substantial numbers remain. At the end of 1981 the Church of England had a total of a little over 16,800 churches. This figure illustrates how well endowed the Church is compared with almost any other voluntary organization in the country. And even if it is accepted, as it should be, that not all of these buildings are in the best location, or of the most convenient size, they do, overall, amount to a range of assets which are difficult to price.

While the Church holds considerable assets at a diocesan level, its main financial assets are held by the Church Commissioners and these stood at almost £1.5 billion in 1982. This figure excludes the value of churches, the value of the land on which they stand, the capital value of parsonage houses and all works of art owned by the Church.

I have left until last in the list of assets the one which is most valuable: its clergy, its Religious and its full-time workers. The Church's paid labour force is very substantial indeed. In 1981 there were 10,985 full-time clergymen. And while this shows a drop from, say, the turn of the century, there are now large numbers of women who wish to, and in my opinion should, have their vocations listed.

Can these substantial resources be used more effectively to support the Church in its national role? In answering this question, three issues need to be considered. These are: how can people learn most easily about Christianity, accepting of course that faith itself cannot be taught? How can the clergy's role in transmitting knowledge about the Christian faith be strengthened? And, finally, can the Church raise the necessary funds to finance the major programme of activities which the answers to the first two questions will entail?

I take the question of finance first. If the income for parishes could be doubled, the Commissioners' income could be released from paying for the salaries of clergy. This is a target which is surely within the realm of possibility, particularly if the laity can be inspired by the Church's attempt to fulfil its evangelizing role.

There is one reason above all else why a major emphasis should be placed on considering the clergy's role and functions. While the support of this group alone will not ensure the redirection of the Church towards its national mission, without their active support and participation it is unlikely that such a change of direction could ever be brought about. I would like to see the clergy assume the responsibilities that Coleridge allocated to the group he called the Clerisy: to safeguard, develop and disseminate the Christian faith and spiritual heritage of the nation.

How can these functions be carried out more effectively today? A prerequisite is the raising of the spiritual and intellectual attainment of the clergy. So how can these two roles best be strengthened? Continual cuts in higher education mean that the Church must focus at present on the second element. The Church can no longer rely on getting its intellectual stimulus from university-based theology departments. The Church should consider building up the academic prowess of a selected number of its own theological colleges. These more highly powered theological colleges should aim to fulfil three objectives. First, to raise the all-round qualification of the students so that they themselves feel more adequately equipped to undertake their role in society along the same lines that Coleridge thought of for his clerisy. Second, for some staff and research students to undertake the research needed to enable the Church to develop its role. Third, to help develop additional skills in the priests to allow them to play a part in the other changes suggested here, particularly the education reforms.

Among the many qualities needed by a successful priest is the ability to teach and to preach. Few young priests can preach and, of those who can, little credit for this goes to their theological college. Given the importance of preaching the Word, it is staggering to learn how little emphasis is placed in developing these skills during a priest's training period. And, while preaching is also one way of teaching, it is not the only one, nor probably the most successful among the young. Developing the skills of the teacher is an issue which theological colleges also need to take on board.

Even the best trained priest, however, will find it difficult to cope with the spiritual problems of an urban environment if the Church insists on squandering one of its most important assets: the parish system. The trend is to supplant parishes with team ministries. But I believe this line of reasoning mistakes the consequence of failure for its cause. Indeed, I would argue that the maintenance of the parish system is crucial to a national Church and, instead of endlessly debating ways of dismantling it, more of the discussion should centre on reforms aimed at helping it perform effectively. Here I believe a number of changes in the education sphere are important. A much greater involvement in education could again begin to give a structure to the priest's working day and, in doing so, help fulfil that other role of the clerisy, namely the dissemination of the faith.

Firstly, theological colleges should develop the teaching skills of priests so that they will be able to perform effectively in the classroom. But, as everybody knows, it is difficult to begin teaching the principles of the Christian faith if young people have not been brought up in a favourable Christian environment. The Anglican Church should therefore consider two further reforms. The first would be to set aside funds so that over a period of time, and together with other denominations, it would become responsible for the training of an ever-growing proportion of all primary school teachers. Teaching the Christian faith would be part of what these training colleges would offer to their students.

At the same time the Church should reverse the decline in the number of church schools, though ensuring that any change should be undertaken sensitively. In the first place, the Church needs to make sure that none of its present schools, and this applies in the main to secondary schools, operates a selection policy which undermines the comprehensive principle. Second, any expansion of the schools should be within the primary school sector. The aim should be to have a church primary school in every parish. In this way – through church primary schools, and greater involvement in all secondary schools – pupils would not only be introduced to the main ideas of the Christian faith, but would also understand what to do in church and would feel at home there. It would have two further advantages. Church primary schools would prepare many of the children for confirmation, which would mean that even if many of them dropped away during adolescence they would always have the faith to come back to. This work in the primary school would give a working structure to the daily round of many an inner-city priest. Such a strategy would also make sure that over time the priest would be known by an ever-growing proportion of his parishioners.

In secondary schools, parish clergy could become part-time chaplains, if only to offer to reach RE after school hours. I know what peer group pressure can be like, but many schools now have thriving society meetings at the end of formal teaching, and this could offer the Church an opportunity to gain an entrance which is welcomed.

These links with the pupils and their families should be built upon whenever contact is made between parishioners and the local church. Here a balance needs to be struck between meeting the needs of the parish at each of the major rites of passage and encouraging parishioners to understand what Christian commitment entails.

Let me give an example of how to adapt practices to the spiritual needs of some parishioners. While many families still turn to the Church when a death occurs, the Church has yet to begin responding adequately to the issue of grieving. How dramatic our failure is on this score was brought home to me in an article by Peter Brotherton in a recent issue of *Portsea Parish News*. He writes:

> A few years ago now I recall attending a meeting of the Oxford Council of Churches at which a minister from the United Reformed Church told us that he had recently preached at the annual service held at the local crematorium for relations and friends of those whose ashes were buried there. He then stunned the whole meeting, clergy and laity from all the main churches in the city, by telling us that no fewer than ten thousand people had attended the service. It was certainly the biggest congregation in England that year.

I would be very surprised if the needs of the people of Oxford were in any way different from those in other parts of the country. Most people would of course find it confusing to attend a requiem on All Souls' Day. But it would be possible for the Church to think about a special service, say on the weekend following All Souls' Day, and inviting all those families who have had a bereavement during the previous year. Contacts could be made immediately following these services which would provide the basis for parish visiting afterwards.

This is just one example of the role 'folk services' could play in an outward-looking Church. The main points in the

Christian year – for example, Christmas, Epiphany, Lent and Easter – should all attract special services. Harvest festivals and Mothering Sundays are also two other times when the Church should be seen to be reaching out and letting it be known that the services will be for the parish and not just the elect.

I have tried to show that remaining in the Anglican fold is as much a reflection of potential as of actuality, and that it is far more a matter of faith, hope and commitment than it is of calculation. I am still an Anglican because it is my home. Even though the Church of England is a fractured fellowship and alienated in many ways from the community it strives to incorporate, I believe it has the resources to emerge from its own dark night and fulfil the mission God has entrusted to it. And so it is where I shall remain.

This chapter is based on the Bevir Memorial Lecture which I gave at Eton College in 1984 and I wish to thank the Headmaster for extending this invitation to me. Many of the ideas set out here came from conversations with the Rev. Perry Butler. Neil McIlwraith commented on the text of that lecture and Kay Andrews on its redraft as this chapter. My secretary, Joan Hammell, typed both versions and I am grateful to all four people for their help.

CONCLUSION

John V. Taylor

SIX VERY DIFFERENT PEOPLE have given their considered reasons for belonging to the Church of England. That's a change!

There was a time, and not so long ago, when anyone who was not sure how to describe his or her beliefs was automatically labelled 'C of E'. Today it is those unconvinced and uncommitted who form the largest 'denomination' in our country and are quite content to carry no religious tag. So it is natural that Tommy Dingsdale, who of all the six writers most clearly represents what he calls the 'real world', should answer the question 'Why I am still an Anglican' as though it were the more fundamental 'Why I am a Christian'. In the context of our 'real world' he's right, of course, and the niceties of our arguments about one denomination or another are growing more glaringly irrelevant as time moves on. I am reminded of an English tourist who, on arriving at Madras airport, was being helped by an Indian immigration officer to fill in his entry form.

'Religion?' he was asked.

'Christian.'

'Yes, I am sure you are Christian, but which damnation?'

However, while the divisions and exclusions persist among Christians, it is an important step towards mutual appreciation when people begin seriously to examine their reasons for adhering to this rather than that Church. In the first place it is a helpful courtesy towards those of other traditions who want to understand rather than condemn and are looking for an interpreter. I shared the essays in this book, even before I had read them myself, with a French Roman Catholic who has prayed and worked for the unity of the churches for nearly thirty years, and she found that even the somewhat contradictory mixture of arguments took her further into the understanding she is continually seeking. But even more important is the self-understanding that comes from trying to give a reason for one's attachment to a particular branch of the world-wide Church. Only the unthinking can persist in the belief that their tradition alone holds the truth, entire and flawless. The very exercise of asking why this rather than that is the right way *for me* opens one's mind to the possibility that it might not be. Indeed, halfway through one of these essays, I began to think that the writer hadn't a good word to say about the Church of England! But the truest adherence to a tradition is that which sees its blemishes and longs for them to be corrected. This critical loyalty, under the enlightenment of the Holy Spirit, is what enables the universal Church to be *semper reformanda*, under continuous reform.

Moreover, by recognizing and bringing to the surface one's real reasons for loving and belonging to one Christian tradition, one perceives that every such allegiance has a relative, not an absolute, claim, and this enlarges one's appreciation of those for whom a different way is right. Or, to put it very simply, it is encouraging to find that when six very different people say publicly why they prefer the Church of England not one of them speaks arrogantly or dogmatically.

This suggests powerfully that the most effective ecumenism will be achieved not by the self-effacement of the separated traditions, but by self-sharing. And I do not mean self-assertion. The most creative stance we can adopt in our relationships with one another ecumenically is not 'These are our own claims', but 'This is what we are, for better or worse, and these are the reasons why we have become what we are. Now, help us understand what you are.' If this book demonstrates such a stance in very personal terms, as I believe it does, it should be taken as a pointer that could lead the Churches into more effective dialogue and co-operation.

One reason why I am sure this is the right way forward is that eventually we are going to have to take that way in our inter-faith relations with those of our countrymen who are Jews, Muslims, Hindus, Sikhs or Buddhists. Here again we seek neither self-assertion nor self-effacement. It will not be a matter of advertising our claims but of presenting and sharing our selves – what we are and why we have become what we are. At this moment we cannot foresee the outcome of such a meeting of contradictory convictions, but we need not fear it. For, as Roger Hooker has said in his essay:

> I need to enter into beliefs that are different from mine to discover what my own are. In this kind of encounter the Christian can begin to discover afresh who Christ is and what it means to follow him.

> *John V. Taylor*